Praise for Peter Wylie and
Baseball, Fundraising, and the 80/20 Rule

"PETER WYLIE, a frequent contributor to fundraising conferences and a forerunner in applying statistical reasoning to advancement, does an excellent job of showing why we should care about taking a disciplined, scientific approach to the data already at our disposal—because it can make our development operations more effective at securing private support of our schools and organizations. This collection of essays would be a valuable addition to any fundraiser's bookshelf." —*Robert D. Scott, executive director of development services, Massachusetts Institute of Technology*

"HAVING READ Peter Wylie's new book, it occurred to me that while some of us may think that analyzing donor data is as enjoyable as a traffic jam, the benefits of acquiring a thorough knowledge of our donor records is well worth the time spent. We as annual fund managers, major gift officers, planned giving officers, prospect researchers, and call-center managers should be very excited about this growing area. We can dazzle our managers with an increased knowledge of our constituents, resulting in ever-greater gifts." —*Catherine Heist, research analyst, Arizona State University Foundation, and member chair, APRA-Arizona*

"PETER WYLIE has a gift for making data mining fun! This book is a journey of discovery and redefines how to go about data mining. The additional notes from Peter give an amazing insight to what he was thinking and what he would like to add. It's a great read!" —*Paulette L. Butterworth, research associate, Southwestern University*

"PETER WYLIE'S work brings a much-needed element of science to advancement, and I've become a real advocate for his brand of predictive modeling. It's about making better decisions. Who wants to spin your wheels on the wrong prospects?" —*Brandon Ferris, director for school advancement, Saint George's School (Wash.)*

"WHEN IT COMES to data mining for institutional advancement, Peter Wylie was—and still is—in the vanguard. He demonstrates that you don't need arcane methods to extract actionable information from your data. What you need is incisive, straightforward data analysis. Peter is a master at making data analysis user-friendly. If you want to get the best return from your donor database—and understand how you did that—keep this book close at hand."

—*Paul F. Velleman, associate professor of social statistics,*
Cornell University, and author of Intro Stats.

"I FOUND Peter Wylie's book a very insightful read. We have been using both data mining and predictive modeling for several years, and I have found Peter's work to be very insightful, both reinforcing our thinking and providing wonderful nuggets of information to help us improve. The content is valuable not just to prospect research and analysis, but to all parts of the advancement from annual fund and phone center calling to strategic thinking about fundraising and campaign management."

—*August R. Freda Jr., director of development research,*
University of Notre Dame, and chapter president, APRA-Indiana

"WITH DEVELOPMENT BUDGETS shrinking and expenses going up, everyone in the field is more aware of the value of data mining. But even so, the data very often just sit there. Working with Peter has given our department a way we can do something creative with our data to boost all our programs."

—*Stephanie Jewell, development research analyst, Ohio Wesleyan University*

"I'VE JUST FINISHED reading Peter Wylie's new book, and have to say, I'm once again inspired by data mining. I enjoyed this book, which is saying a lot for a book on data, and would recommend it to anyone who believes in data mining and recommend it even more to those who don't. This book will make you a believer." —*Karen Maki, associate director, research,*
University of British Columbia, and president, APRA-Canada

"IT WAS WITH great trepidation that I agreed to review Peter Wylie's new book. After all, what I knew about data mining could probably fill a thimble. I was assured that this new book was geared for the data mining-challenged personnel such as myself. And it was!! —*Carla Goring-Madden,*
consultant, CGM Research

"THIS EASY-TO-READ collection of articles by Peter Wylie provides several clear examples of how data mining and modeling at even the most basic level can enhance an organization's effectiveness. Anyone interested in making a case for bringing data analysis to his or her organization can find plenty of justification in this book. It's written in a way that everyone—from the least technically inclined but experienced fundraiser to the new-to-advancement statistician—will understand. Finally, through Peter's historical framing of his work, he not only draws a map of his own data mining journey, but he points toward a promising future of analytical paths." —*Audrey Geoffroy, data analyst,*
University of Florida Foundation

"AS A PROSPECT RESEARCHER, I am always looking for ways to find new prospects, and Peter Wylie's book presents a number of interesting ways to do so. It is eye-opening to discover what valuable information is contained in any alumni database. I am looking forward to trying out these formulas on my own database. Peter entertainingly shows how serious analysis of data can very quickly yield impressive results: By focusing on the prospects with the greatest likelihood of giving, money is better spent and the return on a smaller investment can be much greater. Perhaps the most important message I learned from this book is that data mining is not only something any development office can do but also is something every development office *should* do."
—*George Kopec, development research and records manager,*
Ogelthorpe University, and president, APRA-Georgia

"THE NUMBER-ONE ISSUE facing advancement today is that there are more alumni and potential donors than staff can possibly contact. For many schools, the prospects are in a database if you know where to look. In this compilation, Peter Wylie helps advancement professionals understand the necessity of data mining and how to use it in a practical way. Upon first read you will be able to implement techniques that will efficiently lead you to new donors immediately." —*Chris Mueller, client consultant, advancement services, Stamats*

Also From CASE

Data Mining for Fund Raisers: How to Use Simple Statistics to Find Gold in Your Donor Database (Even if You Hate Statistics) *by Peter B. Wylie*
Written in a lively and practical manner, this book guides you through eight essential steps that illustrate how to apply statistics to achieve better outcomes.
CASE 2004. 7 x 10 softcover. 90 pages. Item 28208.
$36.95 CASE members/$48.95 nonmembers

KeyDonor: Multimedia Course in Data Mining for Fundraising Professionals
by Peter B. Wylie and Data Description
A training course on CD designed to make Wylie's expert advice available to you and your colleagues in a self-paced, distance-learning environment. It's a day-long predictive modeling workshop, ready when you are.
Data Description 2006. CD-ROM. Item 28410.
$459 CASE members/$475 nonmembers

Advancement Services: A Foundation for Fundraising, 2nd ed., *edited by John Taylor*
This updated edition is all-new and expanded to cover the ground of this important profession.
CASE 2007. 7 x 10 softcover. 320 pages. Item 28239.
$46.95 CASE members/$62.95 nonmembers

A Kaleidoscope of Prospect Development: The Shapes and Shades of Major Donor Prospecting *by Bobbie Strand*
A pioneer in the field of prospect research and development, Strand outlines all you need to know to get started and reach your goals in prospect development.
Coming from CASE in Spring 2008!

Find them all at www.case.org/books

CASE has a range of conferences and workshops covering advancement services, prospect research and development, gift processing, stewardship, and more. Check out www.case.org and click on Conferences for the latest information.

Baseball, Fundraising, and the 80/20 Rule

STUDIES IN DATA MINING

Peter B. Wylie

Council for Advancement and Support of Education (CASE) is the professional organization of advancement professionals at all levels who work in alumni relations, communications, development, and advancement services.

CASE offers high-quality training, information resources, and a wide variety of books and publications for advancement professionals.

For more information on CASE or a copy of our books catalog, visit www.case.org, or call (202) 328-5900.

Book design: Daniel Kohan, Sensical Design & Communication
Art Director: Angela Carpenter Gildner
Editorial Director: Lori A. Woehrle

COUNCIL FOR ADVANCEMENT
AND SUPPORT OF EDUCATION
1307 New York Avenue, NW
Suite 1000
Washington, DC 20005-4701
www.case.org

CASE EUROPE
5th Floor, 5-11 Worship Street
London, EC2A 2BH
United Kingdom

CASE ASIA-PACIFIC
20 Lower Kent Ridge Road
Singapore 119080

Acknowledgments

I WAS PROBABLY 15 YEARS OLD or so when I realized that writing was something I was pretty good at and (sometimes) actually enjoyed doing. If I could do it without boring you to tears, I'd thank a whole bunch of people I haven't seen for a very long time for all the encouragement they gave me with my writing. I won't do that. I also won't bust all the pompous and arrogant individuals who discouraged me from writing—although that part you wouldn't find boring at all.

But let me thank some of the folks who have helped make this book possible:

You readers. You guys have to be first on the list because you keep me at the keyboard. Sometimes it's a thoughtful e-mail you send that says how an article or a book has inspired you to focus on the analytical side of fundraising. Sometimes it's just handing me a book to sign while you're running to make another session at a convention. And sometimes it's all the time and effort you put into a frank and balanced critique of something I've written. Without incidents like that, there is no way I would ever have written this book. No way.

Lori Woehrle. Lori, your dedication to the work you do at CASE always boosts me up. Your fresh ideas on publishing and how to keep doing a better job of serving members is inspiring. And your energy—your energy for your job and that special family of yours has gotten me out of the doldrums of self-pity and complaining more than a few times.

Deb Bongiorno. Deb, you've stretched me intellectually and will continue to do that as long as I still have my marbles. And you laugh at my stupid jokes and lack of PC when you probably shouldn't. But what a joy it is when you do.

Robin Netherton. Robin, whoa! The consummate professional editor! Working with you is great, even when we have our little tiffs. You take all the anxiety out of getting a writing project done on time and done right.

John Sammis. Buddy, you're a great friend and colleague who's always encouraged me in my writing. With your quick and incisive mind you see things I don't see and don't hesitate to bring them to my attention. And you've given me more reasons than I can count not to retire.

Linda Margolis-Wylie. Mommy, you're last on the list here, but you're first in my heart. You've put up with me for almost 33 years when a lot of spouses wouldn't. And you've never done anything but encourage me to write what I wanted to write. I can never thank you enough for that.

Table of Contents

Preface

MY FIRST EXPOSURE TO DATA MINING was about 10 years ago, in
the fall of 1997. But the story actually begins long before that—way back
in the late '60s. I had just gotten my undergraduate degree and had gone
to work for a trade association in Hartford, Connecticut, that did research
for the life insurance industry. It was a cool place. I particularly liked all
the applied psychologists ambling around who'd gotten their doctorates
right after World War II. Unlike the stodgy professors I'd had at college,
these guys were easy to talk to and encouraged my interest in statistics and
research methodology.

They also made it painfully clear I wasn't going to get very far in the field
without a Ph.D. So, after a stay of barely 15 months, I went off to New York
City to Teachers College—Columbia University's school of education. That
was a *truly* cool place: a series of big old buildings constructed in the late 19th
century that housed this bustling intellectual activity, all focused on applied
human behavior. My third or fourth day there, this geeky professor (and such
a nice guy) sat next to me in the sprawling cafeteria with the vaulted ceilings.
He started talking about his work on attention span with children and adults in
classrooms. I didn't fully grasp what he was telling me, but I got enough to walk
away thinking I'd made the right choice to go there.

That semester, and for several semesters after that, I took all the statistics
and methods courses I could cram into my schedule. I loved every one of them,
even though several were poorly taught. I didn't care. This was going to be my
life's work. However, the real world managed to intervene.

■ My extroverted friends did not encourage my interests: "Statistics? That's
boring, and it's not plugged into all the problems out there we need to be
solving. Helping people is what it's all about, man." They made a compelling
case. We had an unbalanced president who was not extracting us from Viet-
nam, and the social justice changes that had begun a few years earlier were

1

slowing to a crawl. Their fervor and the strength of their arguments tugged me away from my passion for data analysis.

■ My major professor appeared on the scene. He was even more passionate than my friends about the social problems of the country. On top of that, he had little interest in the analytical techniques that so fascinated me. Nor did he really understand them. (I did take advantage of his discomfort with things analytical to do my dissertation on a statistical topic—mostly so he couldn't slow me down with his endless obsessing.)

■ Information technology was pretty crude back then. In the late '60s, there were no warp-speed laptops, only slow, bulky computers that required punch cards for data input—horribly cumbersome stuff. And there was not even a glimmer of what the Web would offer us several decades later.

For more than 20 years after grad school, I put the stats aside and focused on an area that I think is enormously important—I call it "organizational marriage counseling." I worked with an extremely talented friend from Columbia. The two of us helped the heads of family-owned businesses (and other privately held companies) iron out their differences in the way a family counselor would with a troubled husband and wife. We had some successes (along with many failures) and managed to write three books about the topic.

But there was a problem: I really didn't like the work. And, truth be told, I didn't have the right temperament, the right make-up for it. Try as I might to fight against the characterological grain, I was too impatient and too judgmental to ever be really satisfied following that path.

Getting off the path was a struggle, but some things had happened that helped ease my way. High-speed, powerful PCs had come along. The Web was getting more and more sophisticated with every passing week. And two guys to whom I'll forever be indebted popped into my life.

The first was John Sammis. I met John in 1993 over the phone when I called his company, Data Description Inc., to find out about a statistics software package it sold. John gave me an excellent price on the package, and I began playing around with it as soon as it arrived in the mail. I was bowled over by the speed and ease with which I could do analysis. I had gotten the data-analysis bug back, big time. Over the years I kept in touch with John. About two years ago, we started working closely together; he has become not only a great colleague but a great friend.

The second was a quirky genius named Bo Schnurr, whom I met just 10 years ago. Bo turned me on to data mining, and I owe him much for that. He opened a door for me—helping educational institutions and nonprofits do a better job of raising money through data-driven decision making. It's a door I don't think I will ever walk back though.

So, here I am doing data mining for universities and nonprofits and having the time of my life with it. I've written a short book on it, *Data Mining for Fund Raisers: How to Use Simple Statistics to Find Gold in Your Donor Database—Even If You Hate Statistics.* If you've read it, you know it covers the basics of data mining and predictive modeling for people who work in development.

This book is a bit different. It includes nine articles I've written on the topic of mining and modeling, some before I wrote the *Data Mining* book, but most afterward. On each of them, I've added a few lines telling you a little about what I was thinking when I wrote it and what I hope you'll get from it.

Here, though, let me tell you why I wrote them:

- I've already said this, but let me say it again. I love this stuff. It keeps me up at night. I never tire of it.

- I like to write. I think it's in my DNA. My grandfather (who died before I could meet him) liked to write and was pretty good at it in spite of the fact he was a physician. (In most cases, doctors don't like to write, nor are they particularly good at it.) Anyway, I think I inherited the trait from him.

- The biggest reason I wrote them is *you*. So many of you have read the things I've written and told me you've found them helpful that it compels me to write more. It really does. I can't thank you enough for your encouragement.

I hope you find this collection of papers interesting and helpful. Whatever you think of them, as always, I would like to get your feedback. Again, I can't tell you how much I appreciate your reading what I write.

Peter Wylie
February 2008

PART I

The Data-Mining Process

Chapter 1

Model Behavior

*Statistical modeling can help you find
the right equation for fundraising success*

Originally published in the April 1999 issue of CASE CURRENTS

Author's note: *This is the first piece I ever wrote for CASE. I composed it in
the fall of 1998, when I knew very little about fundraising in general and educational advancement in particular. As with anything written almost a decade ago,
I would do it differently today . . . but not much differently. What I would change
is the heavy focus of the article on the annual fund. I would put much more
emphasis on the power of data mining for identifying potential donors for major
giving. That's one of the biggest lessons I've learned over the intervening years.
Schools leave too much big campaign money on the table because they ignore the
wealth of internal data they have—data that are just sitting there waiting to be
analyzed.*

WHEN I TELL PEOPLE what I do for a living—statistical modeling for
nonprofits—I usually get one of three reactions: confusion ("What the heck is
that?"), polite prevarication ("Oh, that sounds interesting!"), or humor ("Boy,
that'll keep you up at night!").

If you're a fundraiser with at least a few thousand prospects—and you're
concerned about fundraising's increasing costs and diminishing returns—my
job should interest you, though, because what I do can make your efforts to
reach small- to medium-sized givers more productive.

Even if you don't have the resources to do modeling right away, you should
be aware of it, because it's becoming increasingly important in the nonprofit
fundraising arena. When your colleagues at other, equally worthy nonprofits
start getting a greater share of your alumni's giving dollars, you'll at least understand why.

The Basics

While the actual process of statistical modeling is complicated, the concept is simple. Essentially, it's a way to use information in your alumni-development database to create an equation that predicts who is most likely to respond positively to your appeals. Why is this important? There are at least four reasons:

1. It can make your appeals far more cost-effective. You don't need me to tell you that fundraising appeals (by mail, phone, carrier pigeon, or whatever) are expensive. Just a small increase in the percentage of alumni who respond positively can make all the difference between a successful campaign and one you'd rather forget.

Tables 1.1 and 1.2 give a representative example. They compare direct-mail campaigns for the same group of 100,000 prospects. Each campaign has an average gift of $40 and a per-piece cost of $1. The drop-off rate for subsequent appeals is also the same, 50 percent.

For the campaign run without statistical modeling, the return rate of the first appeal is 5.5 percent. As Table 1.1 shows, the net revenue of the first appeal is $120,000 and the second appeal is $10,000, for a total of $130,000—or 65 cents per piece mailed.

Table 1.2 shows the results after using statistical modeling to segment the database into tenths, or deciles. The top decile is people who have a 10 percent response rate; the bottom decile, those who have only a 1 percent likelihood of responding.

If you mail to only 80,000 prospects (10,000 in each of the first eight deciles) in your first appeal and 50,000 (10,000 in each of the first five deciles) in your second appeal, your net revenue will be $158,000, making your profit per piece $1.21. Presto! By not mailing to people in the deciles where you would lose money, you cut your costs and increase your revenue per piece significantly.

2. You get a potentially high return on a minimal investment. In other words, statistical modeling is not very expensive. Nonprofits waste tens of thousands of dollars by needlessly appealing to bad prospects. If they'd spend a small fraction of that on building a reliable predictive model, they could put the remainder to work finding new prospects or supporting their causes. Incidentally, modeling works with as few as 500 records, so you can do this even at a small campus.

3. You'll know very quickly whether it's working. Statistical modeling will either work or it won't—and you'll get the results right away. Like a baseball

Table 1.1. Mailing to 100,000 prospects without statistical modeling

	Response rate	Responses	Gross revenue (Responses x $40 average gift)	Mailing cost ($1 per piece)	Net revenue (gross revenue – mailing cost)	Revenue per piece mailed (net revenue/ number mailed)
First appeal: 100,000	100,000 @ 5.5%	5,500	$220,000	$100,000	$120,000	$1.20
Second appeal: 100,000	100,000 @ 2.75%	2,750	$110,000	$100,000	$10,000	$0.10
Total		8,250	$330,000	$200,000	$130,000	$0.65

Table 1.2. Mailing to 100,000 prospects with statistical modeling

	Response rate	Responses	Gross revenue (Responses x $40 average gift)	Mailing cost ($1 per piece)	Net revenue (gross revenue – mailing cost)	Revenue per piece mailed (net revenue/ number mailed)
First appeal: 80,000	10,000 @ 10%	1,000	$208,000	$80,000	$128,000	$1.60
	10,000 @ 9%	900				
	10,000 @ 8%	800				
	10,000 @ 7%	700				
	10,000 @ 6%	600				
	10,000 @ 5%	500				
	10,000 @ 4%	400				
	10,000 @ 3%	300				
Second appeal: 50,000	10,000 @ 5%	500	$80,000	$50,000	$30,000	$0.60
	10,000 @ 4.5%	450				
	10,000 @ 4%	400				
	10,000 @ 3.5%	350				
	10,000 @ 3%	300				
Total		7,200	$288,000	$130,000	$158,000	$1.21

player's batting average, a golfer's score for a round of 18 holes, or a stock's performance on the New York Stock Exchange, it's a set of numbers that won't lie.

4. Almost everybody in the for-profit sector is doing it. Statistical modeling may be the new kid on the block in the nonprofit sector, but it's no stranger to the for-profit, direct-marketing world. If you don't believe me, ask someone you know who does marketing for a bank, credit card company, or major retailer. These companies spend enormous amounts on database marketing, and a good chunk of that money goes to building statistical models of who's going to buy what, when, and for how much.

How to make it happen

So how does statistical modeling work, and what type of data does it require? Let's first address skills. To do statistical modeling, you'll need three people with specific skill sets: the fundraising expert, the computer expert, and the modeling expert.

- **The fundraising expert** is the person who knows the donor universe you're trying to reach, has experience in trying to appeal to it, and wants to cut costs and increase revenue. On a campus, this is most likely the annual fund director.

- **The computer expert** is a highly skilled, flexible problem-solver who has experience working with the technical end of many different databases at different organizations. This person could be either a campus employee or a consultant.

- **The modeling expert,** or data miner, is someone who knows how to apply statistical techniques like multiple regression, cluster analysis, and others with equally scary names. This person is more than just familiar with these techniques; he or she can get down and dirty with the database to find the things that differentiate givers from nongivers, sort of like a data detective. This person also could be a consultant or a campus employee.

How it's done

Here is how the process of statistical modeling actually works. In brief, you build a research file, select development and validation samples, identify differentiators, develop a model, validate the model, score your database, and implement and further test your model. Let me elaborate.

1. Build a research file. You do this by selecting a random sample of prospects from your alumni-development database.

I know, I know, your database is a mess and you're in the process of a huge overhaul. But let's be honest—you will never be completely happy with the quality and completeness of your data. That's OK: With information technology advancing at warp speed, tomorrow will always bring a new and better piece of data. But this shouldn't prevent you from acting on the information you have today.

The computer expert can build a "research file"—a relational database that contains all the electronically stored information you have on each prospect in the sample. This information should include every single gift (or lack thereof) from every prospect in the sample as well as all other information you've gathered: age, level of education, class rank, special interests, marital status, occupation, and so on. The more data, the merrier.

2. Draw a development sample and a validation sample. The data miner will divide the prospect records in the research file into two random samples: one for developing the model (the development sample), the other for testing it (the validation sample).

3. Identify differentiators. This is the fun part. The data miner digs through the development sample to find variables that separate the givers from the nongivers.

Some of what the data miner finds will be obvious: Higher-income prospects give more than lower-income prospects; older people give more than younger people. But other variables that affect giving are less predictable. Even something seemingly unimportant, like the presence or absence of a prefix in your name fields, could be meaningful when combined with other variables.

And sometimes the content of the data field is less important than whether the field has anything in it at all. A good example is middle initial. It doesn't matter what middle initial you have for a prospect, but you may find that prospects for whom you have a middle initial are more likely to give than those for whom that field is blank. (I now have an axiom: The more data you have on a person, the more likely that person is to have given.)

The data miner may find as many as 20 variables that show a relationship to giving, although when I'm creating an equation I try to use no more than seven.

4. Develop a model. This is the most technical step—and one you really don't need to understand in detail. The data miner uses a tried-and-true statistical

---

Predicting likelihood of giving: A simplified model

$$y = 0.7x_1 + 0.5x_2 + 0.45x_3$$

y = giving score
x_1 = years since graduation
x_2 = indication of advanced degree (yes/no)
x_3 = indication of employer matching gift program (yes/no)

---

technique (like multiple regression) or maybe a newer technique (like logistic regression or artificial neural networks) to combine the best differentiators into an equation—your model. This equation generates a "likelihood of giving" score for each person in the development sample.

5. Validate the model. Here's where the validation sample comes into play. Using all the data in the validation sample's prospect records except giving history, the data miner uses the equation to assign a "likelihood of giving" score to each prospect. She or he then compares the equation's results to the sample's actual giving history to find out if the equation is accurate or not. (For a very simplified example of what this equation might look like, see the box above.)

6. Score the research file. Once the data miner and fundraising expert agree that the modeling equation works properly, the data miner runs all the records in the alumni database through the equation and assigns a "likelihood of giving" score to each prospect. The computer expert can then transfer these scores into your alumni-development database so you can use this information to segment your appeals.

7. Implement and further test the model. This last step is a bit hazier because you can use the scores from your model in many different ways.

I recommend that you test the scores on your next appeal by comparing them to your prospects' actual giving rates. On average, people with higher scores should be giving more. To check, compute the mean amount given by those prospects who scored in the top 25 percent to that of those who scored in the bottom 25 percent.

Of course, your alumni and prospects are not like catalog customers—you're not going to drop them from your database even if they have almost no likelihood of giving. But you can vary the number and cost of the appeals you make to focus your time, money, and effort on more productive prospects.

The process I've outlined is just the beginning. If statistical modeling is going to help you in the long run, it needs to be part of an across-the-board, database-driven approach to fundraising that's analogous to the for-profit sector's database marketing.

Getting started

Reading this article was the first step. If you're interested in learning more about database marketing as it applies to fundraising, you can do a number of things.

I highly recommend the book *The New Direct Marketing: How to Implement A Profit-Driven Database Marketing Strategy*, by David Shepard Associates, for fundraisers who want to reach small donors. Although the book came out in 1999, it is still relevant and readable. There are also new books on data mining coming out all the time, and if you're interested in the topic—especially if you'd like to make a career of it—you should be checking out these new publications whenever you can. You can also go to seminars, talk with people in the nonprofit world who know more about this stuff than you do, and e-mail me with questions.

If you become a student of this "next wave" in fundraising, your campus will soon reap the benefits—there's no doubt about it.

Ask the Expert
Answers to some questions on statistical modeling

Q: I have a fundraising expert on staff, but where would I find someone to do computer programming or statistical modeling?
A: I strongly recommend that most institutions build some in-house expertise in this area. It will pay off in the long run because that person can continue to dig into your database as it expands—not only in numbers of potential donors but also in more fields that you can use to predict giving.

Many colleges and universities have students, staff members, and faculty members who have both high-level computer expertise and the mathematical know-how it takes to be a good data miner. That's the first place I'd look.

Some smaller campuses and independent schools don't have the budget or personnel to do this in-house, though—and even large institutions might want to use a consultant the first time around. (Make sure the consultant works closely with the staffer you want to train, of course.)

A consultant like myself or a larger firm can get you started. You're not going to find "statistical modeling" in the *Yellow Pages*, though. Look under "database management" or "database marketing."

Q: What characteristics should I look for in a computer expert or data miner?
A: I can think of three:

- **Technical competence.** A consultant or firm should have a good track record of helping nonprofits build useful models. A permanent hire should be someone who's very good at programming and keeps up with the constant changes in the computer field. A good data miner should be computer literate, like to play with numbers, and understand and enjoy statistics and statistical methods.

- **Good interpersonal skills.** Model building is not easy—things often can and do go wrong. Arrogant, intolerant, and inflexible people (no matter how smart they are) only make things worse. Look for people who have a helpful and cooperative attitude.

- **Good verbal skills.** Unfortunately, many smart, technical people are not good at explaining things in understandable terms. When you start looking for consultants or in-house help, pay close attention to how articulate they are when they explain technical stuff to you. If you end up scratching your head, keep looking.

Q: What does it cost?
A: Although many variables can affect the price, you should be able to build a usable model—one that will save you money and generate

significantly more revenue—for less than $20,000. That cost would include:

- the construction of a research file,

- a thorough analysis of the variables in your database that differentiate givers from nongivers,

- the creation of a model (an equation) that efficiently combines these differentiators,

- the application of "likelihood of giving" scores to all prospects in your development database, and

- specific guidelines on how to make the greatest use of those scores for your campus's annual fund and other specific campaigns.

Q: My campus's database contains almost no information on prospects other than name, address, class year, and giving history. Can statistical modeling help me?
A: If you're concerned that there's nothing of predictive value in your database, you can ask a data miner to do a preliminary evaluation for a limited fee. If the person can't find anything of predictive value, then you've spent very little on the effort. But if some potentially useful predictors turn up, you can move ahead with the full project.

You may have more useful data than you realize, though. For example, if I were doing the preliminary evaluation, I might dig into your database and create some easy-to-find yes/no variables for each prospect, such as:

- completed most recent alumni survey,

- e-mail address listed,

- marital status listed, and

- business phone listed.

Then I'd create a "missing data score" for these four variables. A prospect record could have a score of 0 to 4, depending on the number of "yes" answers. Finally I'd produce a table showing how much more the "4s" in your database have given you over the last five years compared to the "0s."

Q: How often should I undertake the modeling process?
A: If you're using an outside consultant, you should get as much mileage as you can out of one model. As long as you have a way of attaching scores to new prospects as they enter your database, your model should remain valid for two to three years.

If someone on your staff is learning to do modeling, you should create an ongoing process. New fields and potentially powerful predictors are creeping into your database all the time. The more a data miner can dig into your database and uncover these gems, the more your overall development efforts will benefit.

Chapter 2

The Many Facets of Data Mining

Fundraising databases are filled
with gems if you know how to dig

Originally published in the September 2001 issue of CASE CURRENTS

Author's note: *I wrote this one in the summer of 2001, before the 9/11 attacks. Almost three years had passed since I'd written the previous article (Chapter 1 in this book). While far from being an advancement expert, I'd learned a lot in those years. In this article I tried to politely, but assertively, make the point that most folks in educational advancement really don't know much about what's in their alumni databases, nor do they realize the substantial predictive power all that information holds. Six years later, I still think that's true. Perhaps the change has been that more people in advancement are now aware of what they don't know about their alumni that they could gather from their databases. What are they doing about that awareness? That's another issue.*

Another suggestion I made in this article is that advancement offices should strongly consider hiring a data analyst whose primary responsibility is foraging through the database to find predictors of giving and to build models that will save money and generate more revenue on appeals. While that suggestion has been far from wholeheartedly embraced, I'm happy to report that a number of schools have hired such professionals. All the ones I've talked to seem very capable and very motivated. And that, I think, is a very good thing.

IN APRIL 1999, MY CURRENTS ARTICLE "Model Behavior" explained how data mining and predictive modeling can help fundraisers conduct more productive annual fund drives. While these concepts often make people furrow their brows, nod off, or whisper snide comments, the article stirred some interest among CURRENTS' readers. Since then, I have received quite a few telephone calls and e-mails about data mining. I have conducted seminars on the topic and worked closely as a volunteer and a consultant with a dozen or so colleges and universities to teach them these techniques. I've had a ball playing around with mountains of data, and I've had a chance to work with a bunch of dedicated people. Throughout this time I've gained three notable insights about education advancement:

1. Most development officers don't realize the value of the information in their databases.

2. When put to use, this information can have powerful implications for both annual and major giving programs.

3. To make that happen, development offices will increasingly require in-house expertise in data analysis.

This article explores these thoughts in greater detail.

Hidden information

I often begin my work with development officers by listing 10 key database questions and asking them how many they could answer immediately, or at least within a half-hour. Most officers say they'd need more than 30 minutes to find the answers. Some might even need weeks, depending on their backlog of report requests.

Fundraisers want answers to lots of questions. What's so special about my 10? By pondering these questions, fundraisers can begin to grasp the richness and power of the information in their databases. Take a look at questions one through four:

1. What percentage of the people in your database have never given you a penny in voluntary support? I used to be shocked when development people couldn't answer this question right off the bat, but then I realized that our perspectives were different.

Development officers are often thinking about short-term horizons—meeting an annual giving target or a seven-year campaign goal. They can tell you what percentage of the database gave to the annual fund last year, or what percentage is likely to support the campaign, but overall giving is not even on their radar screens.

Typically, 50 percent to more than 80 percent of the records in an institution's advancement database are those of people who have never made a gift. Knowing who they are is important because people who have *never* made a gift—especially if they're not recent graduates—are fundamentally different from those who've given you *something*, even if it was just $10 a decade ago. To solicit them in the same way as givers becomes more and more of a losing proposition as time passes. Most institutions I've worked with realize this and don't go after these types for the annual fund very frequently because they know it's not worth the cost of the stamp. Past donors, if they're alive and have their wits about them, are more likely to give again—and that next check might be for a lot more than a sawbuck.

Some development officers believe they should keep in touch with alumni, even if they've never given, just in case they have a change of heart late in life. This approach has some intuitive appeal, even if evidence of its wisdom is lacking. But keeping in touch is different from making repeated annual fund appeals that are likely to go unanswered—and may even alienate these people.

2. What percentage of your donors account for 95 percent of the gifts your institution receives? Most development officers have heard of the "80-20 rule." An Italian economist named Pareto developed this theory of time management about 100 years ago. He claimed that 80 percent of the value of any list of items comes from only 20 percent of those items. If you've got a list of 10 things to do, for example, you can probably achieve 80 percent of the total value by doing only the two most important tasks.

Fundraisers have long applied the same general principle to their work, but today the ratio is closer to 95-5. I'd bet that 95 percent of the money ever given to your institution has come from about 5 percent of the people in your database. I might be off by a point or two, but you get the idea: A relatively small group of people deserve special attention. Think of them as your "best customers."

3. Where do most of your alumni live? Where do most nonalumni donors live? Nonalumni donors very likely live close to your institution. Your alumni probably are more geographically dispersed. Knowing where most of your good prospects live has huge implications for planning events at your institution and at other venues and for deploying development officers. Why spend time and money on expensive travel if the best prospects are within a comfortable drive of campus?

4. What percentage of your alumni have attended at least one institutional function since graduation? You probably haven't seen half of your alumni since the day they received their diplomas. Their level of giving will be dramatically lower than those who've attended even one event. But those who've attended two or more functions, especially if they're in their 20s and 30s, are worth your special care and feeding. The evidence on this is unequivocal: At every single institution I've examined, this group not only gives at a higher rate than others, it also gives greater amounts—even when you hold time since graduation constant. For example, at Queen's University in Ontario, nearly 60 percent of alumni who have attended four or more events are in the university's top 5 percent of lifetime donors. If an alumnus has shown this level of interest within a few years of graduation, careful nurturing could lead to large gifts in later years.

Little things mean a lot

Questions five through eight help me make an important point about data analysis: The existence or absence of data in a field can be as important as—or more important than—what the field contains.

5. Is there a marked difference among the giving rates of people listed in your database with the prefixes Mrs., Ms., and Mr.? If this question seems inane to you, just humor me by looking at what percentage of people with each prefix have given at least $1,000. You might be surprised. At other nonprofits, those with prefixes attached to their records almost always have given more than those without prefixes. At colleges and universities, this field has fewer gaps— almost every record has a prefix attached. Interestingly, a campus database I recently examined showed that those with the prefix "Mrs." had given an average of 3.5 times as much as those with another prefix or no prefix in that field. At another campus, the breakdown by prefix of donors who had given $1,000 or more was as follows: "Mr.," 6 percent; "Ms.," 2 percent; "Mrs.," 11 percent.

6. What percentage of your alumni records contain information about at least one family member other than the alumnus? In every single database I've examined with a field for this information, those with any data listed about a family member had given markedly more than those without such data listed. The same holds true for questions seven and eight:

7. What percentage of alumni have a business telephone number and address listed in your database?

8. What percentage of alumni have an e-mail address listed in your database? Does knowing the answers to detailed questions like these really help a development officer determine if an alumnus is likely to be a donor? Based on my recent experience, the answer is yes. In each case, alumni records that contained information in these fields were likely to have a history of giving.

There's an important difference between correlation and causality, however. Don't spend your time and money collecting information just to fill up each field. Statistical modeling can't tell you why two pieces of data are correlated, but you don't need to know why to make use of that knowledge.

I was able to prove this point when, for a presentation at CASE's Annual Conference for Institutionally Related Foundations, several foundation officers volunteered to let me analyze their databases. I ended up working with the University of Minnesota Foundation, East Carolina University, and Oklahoma State University.

Each test institution was preparing a different type of annual giving initiative. Minnesota was planning a mail campaign to approximately 40,000 alumni, OSU was about to conduct a phonathon to nearly 2,500 alumni who had not made gifts in the previous year, and ECU was developing a phonathon aimed at about 12,500 alumni.

Because of the differences in solicitation efforts, staff availability, and database types, the data-mining process varied somewhat at each institution, but it generally followed five steps: (1) choosing which data fields to include in the project, (2) building a sample file, (3) mining the data, (4) building models, and (5) testing.

For each record in the sample file we examined about five variables, asking one yes-or-no question for each. A "yes" answer received a score of one; "no," a zero. Typical questions were "Does this record have a business phone number listed?" and "Did this alumnus graduate before 1972?" Each record in the sample ended up with a total score between 0 (all answers were "no") and 5 (all answers were "yes"). We stored the scores in a separate file to use once each initiative had ended.

The scores proved to be effective indicators of giving at all three institutions. Higher scores correlated with higher giving rates and larger gifts, just as we had hoped. At the University of Minnesota, for example, 0.2 percent of those who received a score of 0 made gifts, compared to 8.6 percent of those who received a score of 5. (See Figure 2.1.) Interestingly, more than 55 percent of the 40,000 alumni in the sample received scores of 0 or 1.

The total cost for a direct mail campaign can be more than 60 cents per person, so you can see how wasteful it is to mail to alumni who score at low levels. The better approach is to focus on alumni who score 2, 3, or higher, which is the university's strategy for a second mailing (and possibly a third) before its fiscal year closes.

Figure 2.1. University of Minnesota alumni: Percentage giving gifts, by score

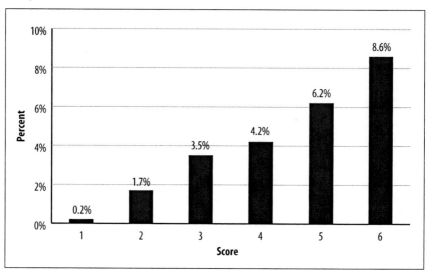

Implications for major gifts

In my first CURRENTS article, I said that data mining and statistical modeling can make an institution's efforts to reach small- to medium-sized givers more productive. But I think these concepts have applications for major gifts as well. Consider my final two questions:

9. What percentage of alumni received their first degree from your institution in each decade, from the 1990s back to the 1930s?

10. At what age do alumni appear to increase their rate of giving? I selected five institutions whose databases I've worked with for the past several years. The five are a mix of public, private, large, and small campuses. For each, I drew a representative random sample of several thousand records from the entire database and looked at data on four variables: whether the alumnus had (1) given $1,000 or more, (2) listed a business telephone number, (3) noted an e-mail address, and (4) was 52 or older. The patterns of giving among all five institutions were uniform and clear. The higher the total score for variables 2 through 4, the more likely the donor was to have made a $1,000-plus gift. (See Figure 2.2.)

Now step back from the data a little. Imagine you're responsible for major giving at your institution and you've just enhanced a portion of your records

Figure 2.2. Percentage of donors giving $1,000 or more, by score

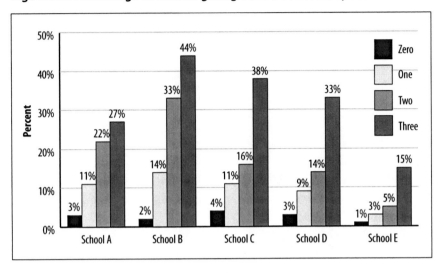

with data from a consulting firm with an excellent reputation for providing accurate information about donors who are capable of making major gifts. You identify 500 of your highest rated alumni who've not yet made a major gift and assign the records a score of 0, 1, 2, or 3 based on whether they include a business telephone number or an e-mail address and represent alumni who are 52 or older.

You not only have a fix on donors who have the capability to give, but you also have a fix on those who are likely to give. The possibilities of saving money and generating more revenue—lots more—are exciting.

Inside expertise

Most academic institutions have an information technology staff that is responsible for maintaining their alumni-development databases. The most talented and dedicated IT staffers are enormously valuable and extremely hard to replace.

As integral as these professionals are to development, your offices need another kind of professional who has related but different responsibilities and skills. You need in-house data analysts who can enter a database, pull out a representative sample, and rapidly scrutinize the data to get answers, as I did in the examples above.

Return to the 10 questions I posed throughout this article. If you had a data analyst on staff, finding answers quickly to questions like those—plus myriad others—would be a piece of cake.

I am realistic about this proposal, however. Building this kind of specialty in fundraising (education or otherwise) is not going to happen right away. I've been pushing the idea for several years and haven't made much headway. Many vendors that provide data analysis products and services resist the idea, as do fundraisers who wonder how one staff person can be as effective as an entire consulting firm. Four clarifications are worth noting and might help convince the skeptics:

Data analysts will not replace prospect-screening vendors. The number of vendors that provide high-quality enhancements to existing databases and create sophisticated predictive models is going to increase. To not take advantage of such products and services—which can supplement, not duplicate, in-house analysis—would be foolish.

Only an insider can take charge of the data analysis "big picture." Consultants, by their very nature, are specialists. It's hard for us to see every institution's big picture. Even if you've purchased an excellent predictive model and high-quality enhancement for a portion of your database, a consultant can't know how and when you should best use that data. Only a knowledgeable staff person can help you decide how to take maximum advantage of what you've bought.

Without an inside specialist, the data-enhancement products and services you purchase are less likely to be used effectively. Let me make this point with a blunt question: In the past five years, have you spent more than $25,000 on enhancing your database with estimates of wealth, capacity to give, and so on, only to have the information untapped and unused by your development officers? Why buy the stuff if you're not going to use it? An inside data analyst can not only help you use data effectively, he or she also can be a persistent thorn in your side until you do use it.

A good data analyst is worth the effort and cost of creating a new position. The cost of creating a new position, even one that's part-time, is a major undertaking. Here are a few suggestions:

- **Be patient.** You need to convince yourself that hiring a data analyst is a good idea before going to the powers that be and asking for funding.

- **Gather evidence.** Find out how an inside data analyst really can help you before you ask for a position. The best way to do this is to identify someone who works with or for you and encourage him or her to take seminars, read books and articles on the topic, and work on a few projects. There's nothing like having one of your own people uncover a startling, hidden fact to make a believer of you and everyone else.

- **Weigh cost and benefits.** You'll easily recoup the costs of salary and benefits by unearthing just one huge donor who wouldn't have been discovered unless your inside data analyst had "mined" them.

PART II

Identifying Donors

Chapter 3

Deep Pockets

Where the alumni money is

Originally published in 2005 on www.case.org

Author's note: *I put this white paper together in the summer of 2003. By that point, I was learning more and more about electronic wealth screening and the heavy emphasis prospect researchers put on getting "outside" data on people in their databases. What was particularly apparent to me was how screening vendors were either missing a lot of people, or they were providing sketchy or inaccurate information on some people. (Since then, I've learned how hard it is for the screeners to find wealth information on people, and that their business is indeed a tough one. For more about that, see Chapter 9.)*

At any rate, what motivated me to write this piece were some distinct patterns I was seeing in almost all the higher-education data I was plowing through: The lion's share of the alumni money was coming from people over about age 55 who had certain codes in the marital-status field. My logic was (and still is): "Are we ignoring that simple fact while we spend oodles on this outside screening stuff? That doesn't seem like a good idea."

I SPEND FROM 10 PERCENT to 20 percent of my work week exhorting (sometimes haranguing) university advancement officers to look in their databases for information that will help them raise more money. I'm sure I sound much like a Sunday morning TV evangelist.

For you, I may be preaching to the choir. If so, you're either a student I've taught to mine your own database, or you're champing at the bit to be taught (or to teach yourself). But most likely you're among the unconverted. And it's for you (especially if you work in the major giving arena) that I've gathered the evidence you'll see rolled out in the next several pages. I hope you'll find it thought-provoking, maybe even compelling.

Where this idea came from

Tracing the provenance of an idea is a bit like doing epidemiology; it's tricky, and often you don't ever figure it out. But as best as I can put it together, this one came primarily from two observations.

1. Certain patterns appear consistently across college and university donor databases. Teaching data mining is a second career for me, and I haven't been at it all that long—a little over five years as of this writing. In that half a decade or so, I've had a chance to pore over representative samples of close to 40 college and university databases. Looking at these collections of information has been fascinating. Each has had its distinctive personality in terms of overall giving levels, overall participation rates, geographical location of most of the alumni, and on and on. But for all these databases, at least two patterns seem invariant:

- The older alumni give disproportionately more than younger alumni.

- There are large differences in the giving rates among the various codes in the marital-status field.

When you combine these two pieces of information—how long people have been out of school, and what their marital status is—it's easy to see where there are *huge* pockets of giving for any representative sample of alumni.

2. Major gift officers are unaware of these patterns and don't take advantage of them. I have a lot of respect and fondness for the "troops" in university advancement: the annual funders and prospect researchers who do the foundation building that eventually leads to major giving. But I must admit to getting a bit frustrated at how unaware they are of some basic patterns in their databases that I know could help them.

Truth be told, I spend more time trying to help prospect researchers than I do annual funders. And with them I get particularly frustrated over their tendency to go to the "outside" (via the Internet and vendors) to find out where the big money is, when I think the answer—at least a lot of it—resides in their own databases, where it's easily (and cheaply) accessible.

Proving my point

Okay, so I was frustrated. I wanted to show you there are big pockets of money (both actual and potential) in your database.

Figure 3.1. Percentage distribution of giving by marital status and class-year quartile for School A

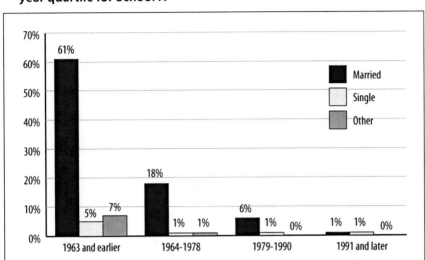

Here is what I did. I picked eight four-year institutions that differ greatly in terms of size, affiliation (public versus private), and student population served. For each institution I had a random sample of at least 5,000 records from the entire alumni database. (I did not include other constituencies like parents, friends, faculty, etc.) And for each record, I had information on (a) total giving, (b) preferred year of graduation, and (c) whatever was in the marital-status field.

From these data I constructed eight graphs. Let me walk you through the graph for School A (see Figure 3.1).

If you look at the graph, several facts will jump out at you:

- The oldest 25 percent of alumni (those who graduated in 1963 or before) account for almost three-quarters (73 percent) of the total alumni dollars given.

- Alumni who are listed in the database as being married account for a huge amount (86 percent) of the total alumni dollars given.

- The youngest 50 percent of alumni (those who graduated in 1979 or later) account for only 9 percent of the total alumni dollars given. (All percentages have been rounded to the nearest hundredth; "0 percent" means that the actual percentage for that group is less than 0.5 percent.)

Now here's what I'd recommend. Browse through the graphs I've constructed for the remaining seven schools (Figures 3.2–3.8). After you do that, I'll catch up with you at the end of the graphs for a little discussion.

Figure 3.2. Percentage distribution of giving by marital status and class-year quartile for School B

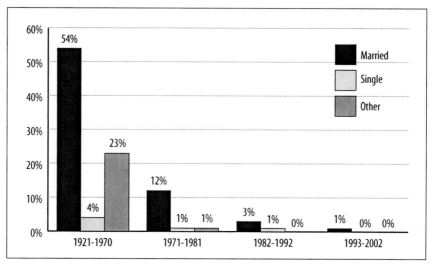

Figure 3.3. Percentage distribution of giving by marital status and class-year quartile for School C

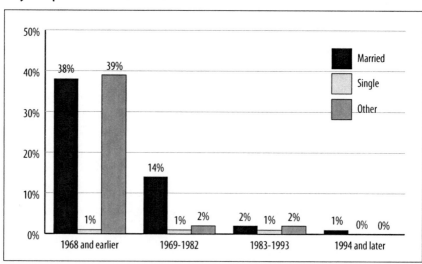

Figure 3.4. Percentage distribution of giving by marital status and class-year quartile for School D

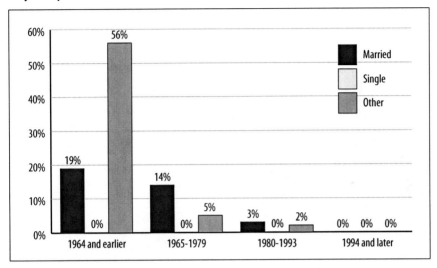

Figure 3.5. Percentage distribution of giving by marital status and class-year quartile for School E

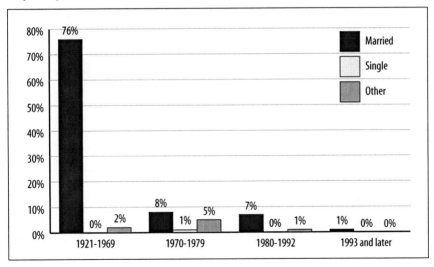

Figure 3.6. Percentage distribution of giving by marital status and class-year quartile for School F

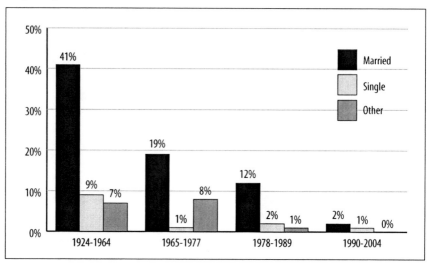

Figure 3.7. Percentage distribution of giving by marital status and class-year quartile for School G

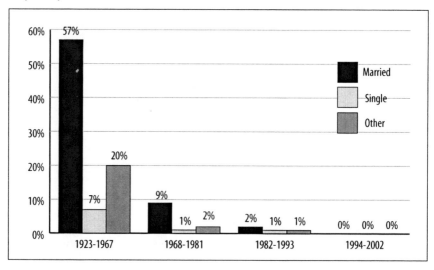

Figure 3.8. Percentage distribution of giving by marital status and class-year quartile for School H

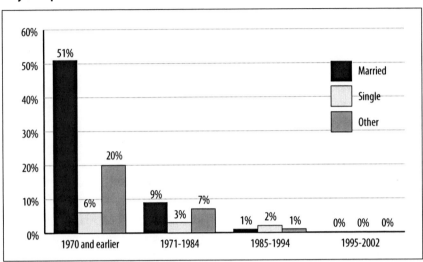

Some discussion

Let's assume these eight schools are reasonably representative of four-year institutions across the country. (I can't, of course, tell you the names of these schools, nor can I even offer descriptions of them. But if I could, I think you'd agree—they are a good "swatch.")

Here are some facts:

■ At least 90 percent of the money from any alumni population tends to come from people who've been out of school at least 30 years.

■ Regardless of their *actual* marital status, alumni listed as married in the database tend to give much more money than alumni with any other marital code, especially if that code is "single."

■ Alumni who have been out at least 30 years *and* are listed as married often give a huge amount of money compared to any other group classified by marital status and class year. (Schools C and D are an exception to this pattern, but even with these institutions, the older "marrieds" are kicking in a lot of money.)

Well, this is all very interesting, right? But what implications do these data have for what prospect researchers and gift officers do? I'm not completely sure; I'm still relatively new to academic advancement, *and* I'm a specialist. And (paraphrasing Abraham Maslow) specialists tend to be like the guy whose only tool is a hammer; he tends to see every problem as a nail.

Nonetheless, here's what I would suggest:

If you're looking for big money from your alumni, *go after people who've been out for at least 30 years.* Going after younger folks for the big bucks seems to make much less sense. Now, I do not mean you should not *nurture* younger alumni, who may well give you a lot of money once they pass 50, better yet once they pass 55. For example, alumni still in their 20s who have given a small amount and have attended a reunion should *definitely* be nurtured. (But that's a whole other topic.)

When it comes to prospect research (both vendor screenings and the individual kind involving the Internet and libraries), I would focus on the older folks. They're much more likely to have the *capacity* to make a big gift than the younger crowd. (If that's what you're already doing, great. But the vast majority of prospect researchers I talk to simply can't make that claim.)

If you want a simpleminded strategy for bringing in *new* major givers among your alumni, here's what I'd do. I'd identify people who are over 55, are listed as married, have a high capacity rating, and have already given some money but not a lot. I think a lot of them are simply waiting for the big ask, even if they're not aware of it.

Chapter 4

A Simple Score

A few data points from your own records can lead you to your best prospects

Originally published in 2005 on www.case.org

Author's note: *Move the clock forward a couple of years to 2005. By that point I had been able to look at upwards of a hundred alumni databases from a wide variety of higher-education institutions—small and large, public and private, non-sectarian and faith-based, urban and rural. Regardless of the differences among these schools, I was seeing a dominant trend in the data I had foraged through. Five very basic pieces of information (contained in just about any school's alumni database) could be combined into a simple score that could be used to segment appeals for the annual fund and major giving. The evidence was incontrovertible.*

Since I wrote this article, John Sammis of Data Description Inc. and I have found that by using a statistical technique called multiple regression, you can create an even more accurate algorithm than the unweighted score described here. This fact adds more fuel to my exhortative fire when I talk to schools about analyzing their data.

OVER THE YEARS I'VE BECOME an avid mystery fan. Though their subject matter can be gruesome, I find them wonderfully distracting and more than a little entertaining. What I find especially intriguing is the mileage detectives can get out of smidgens of evidence. Maybe it's a partial fingerprint or a tiny piece of tissue that contains just enough DNA to be linked to a suspect. Maybe it's a worn tire or running shoe impression that matches the findings from a search warrant. Those little pieces of evidence can shut down violent criminals whose rampages might otherwise persist for decades.

So, what does my taste for mysteries have to do with fundraising? Well, I'm not a cop—probably a good thing for both society and criminals. But I do see myself as a detective in the data-mining and predictive-modeling work I do for higher education. I've gotten pretty good at finding little pieces of information in databases that point to which alumni are most likely to give and which are not.

What I want to do here is talk about how (with the help of your IT staff) you can combine five basic pieces of information into a score that will help you save money and generate more revenue—especially if you work with the annual fund.

Specifically, I'll:

- describe the five pieces of information,

- show how these data can be combined into a simple score,

- show how this score works for 10 different higher-education institutions, and

- talk about how you can use the score in your own school.

The five pieces of information

The five pieces of information that go into making up this score are pretty straightforward:

1. whether a home phone is listed for a record in the database,

2. whether a business phone is listed for a record,

3. whether an e-mail address (either personal or business) is listed for a record,

4. whether a record falls into either the oldest or youngest 25 percent of alumni, and

5. whether a record has the value "missing" or "single" listed in the marital status field.

Why these pieces of information? What's so special about them? Over the years, as I foraged through alumni databases for good predictors of giving, these were the variables that popped up again and again.

Let's work through some examples with several of these pieces of information.

1. Whether a home phone is listed. Figure 4.1 shows the percentage of alumni at a large university who fall at three different levels of lifetime giving: nothing, $1–$74, and $75 or more. (By the way, if you're surprised at how poor this giving picture looks, take a look at what it is for your own school. You may be in for a bit of a shock.)

Figure 4.1. Percentage of alumni at three levels of lifetime giving

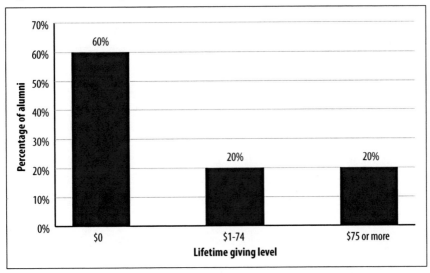

Figure 4.2. Percentage of alumni at three levels of lifetime giving, by presence of home phone number in record

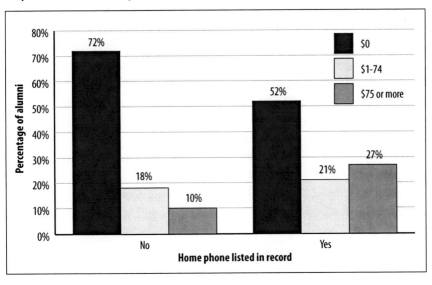

Figure 4.2 shows the difference in the percentages at each of these three levels of giving for alumni who have a home phone number listed in the database versus those who don't. Clearly, alumni who have a home phone listed are better givers than those who don't. Of those with a home phone listed, 48 percent

have given something to the university (however little). Of those without a home phone listed, only 28 percent have given anything.

Before moving on to another example, let's deal with a question I often get when I speak at professional meetings on data mining and predictive modeling: "Wait a minute. Aren't people with a home phone listed more likely to be givers simply because we can reach them by phone? And also because they're more likely to give us their phone numbers when they make a gift? Aren't we talking about a spurious correlation here?"

It's a good question, and I'm always glad when it gets asked. Here's how I respond: Frankly, we don't know how those numbers got in there. If you were to go to your IT staff and ask them to identify (for each record) how the telephone number got into the database, they'd throw up their hands in despair. The more outspoken ones would say: "We don't know. Plus it would be a huge waste of our time to try and figure it out!" The truth is, all we know is that it's in there or it isn't.

What's important here is that the presence or absence of the phone number is *not* what I would call a "proxy" for giving. For example, a proxy variable would be "member of the $1,000 Club." Alumni who are members of this club are givers (and good ones at that). Using their membership as a predictor of giving wouldn't make sense; we already know they're givers. But "home phone listed" is not an automatic measure of giving. There are plenty of alumni who have a home phone listed who haven't given a penny. All we know is that alumni with a home phone listed are more *likely* to be givers than alumni without a home phone listed. So, (and this gets to the nub of my argument) if we're going after new donors—those who haven't yet given us a penny—which alumni are our better bets? Those with a home phone listed, or those without a home phone listed?

2. Whether a record falls into either the oldest or youngest 25 percent of alumni. I don't think it's any secret that the longer alumni have been out of school, the more likely they are to have made a gift to the school, and more likely to have made a large one. However, I don't think university advancement officers have a good sense of how disproportionate the giving is between older and younger alumni. You can read more about this phenomenon in Chapter 3, "Deep Pockets." But for now, let's take a look at this trend in two very different schools: one where the level of lifetime giving is high and one where it is quite low.

As you look at Figures 4.3 and 4.4, you'll see that the alumni in Figure 4.3 have given much more than the alumni in Figure 4.4. This is especially the case when you compare the oldest quartiles (the oldest 25 percent) at the two schools. The "oldsters" in Figure 4.3 have given an average of over $7,000 during their lifetimes, whereas their counterparts in Figure 4.4 have given only about $240 in their lifetimes.

Figure 4.3. Mean (average) lifetime giving by class-year quartile at an institution with high giving

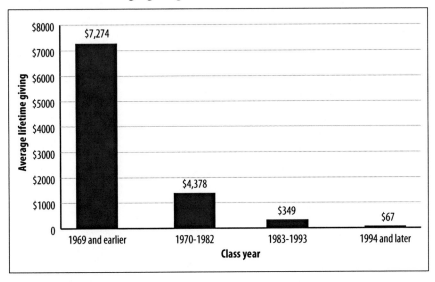

Figure 4.4. Mean (average) lifetime giving by class-year quartile at an institution with low giving

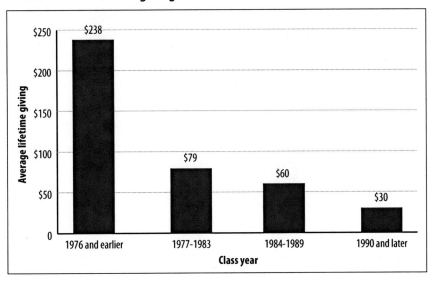

However, when you compare the lifetime giving levels between the oldest and youngest quartiles, there is quite a difference. Admittedly, the difference between the oldest and youngest groups is much greater in Figure 4.3 than in Figure 4.4. If I could show you data from all the schools I've looked at over the years, you'd see that the difference between the oldest and youngest quartiles in Figure 4.3 is much more typical than the corresponding difference in Figure 4.4, and it's probably much more typical of your own institution. But even in Figure 4.4, the oldest alumni have given almost eight times as much (on average) as the youngest alumni.

3. Whether the value "missing" or "single" is listed the marital-status field. When I speak at conferences about data mining and predictive modeling in advancement, people ask me how I discovered the basic predictors I'm laying out in this article. I always hesitate before answering, because the truthful answer is "I'm not exactly sure."

That's the thing about data mining. It's an exploratory process. Sometimes you have a clear idea of what might work as a predictor; sometimes you don't. Sometimes you just stumble onto something. That's what happened with the marital-status field. First I noticed that almost all the four-year institutions I worked with had a marital status field. Then I noticed that for a lot of the records, there was simply no code at all in this field. (I would assign these a code of "missing.") I also noticed that a lot of the records had been assigned a code of "single." When I compared the lifetime giving rate of these "missing" and "single" records with those that had any other code listed, I saw a big difference. The people whose records had other codes, regardless of what they were ("married," "divorced," "widowed," etc.), gave substantially more than the ones listed as "single" or "missing."

To see how pronounced this difference can be, look at Figures 4.5 and 4.6. These graphs show the mean (average) lifetime giving for these two sets of marital codes for two of the 10 schools I looked at for this article.

Combining these pieces into a simple score
Now let's talk about how you can put these five pieces of information together into a score—a score that can eventually be used to save money and generate more revenue on appeals.

We'll get into the details of this in a moment, but first let's confront a reality you may be considering before I even raise it: getting help from your IT staff. Unfortunately, none of the fundraising software I've seen is easy to use when it comes to data analysis. In fact, I think the scale goes from "sort of okay" down

Figure 4.5. Mean (average) lifetime giving by marital code for School 10

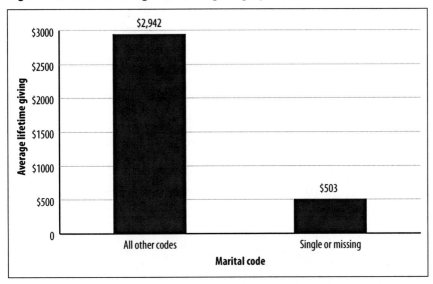

Figure 4.6. Mean (average) lifetime giving by marital code for School 6

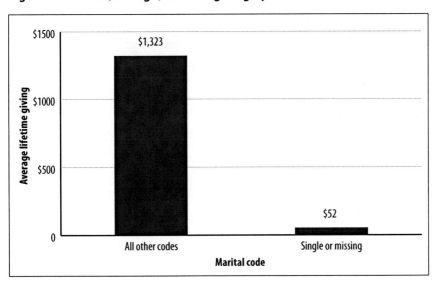

to "terrible." This makes the job of your overworked IT people (the ones who haven't already been lured away by higher-paying jobs in the private sector) all the more difficult.

Keep that in mind when you ask for their help on a project like this. Be persistent, because they'll tend to put tasks like this one on the back burner in favor of all the "urgent" jobs that need to be done in your shop. But be nice and patient and understanding, too.

Probably the best way to start this project is to ask your IT person to pull a random sample of 10,000 "solicitable" alumni records from your database that can be put into an Excel file with the following fields:

- UNIQUE ID NUMBER (the number you use to keep track of all records in your database)

- HOME PHONE LISTED (1 if a home telephone number is listed for the record, 0 if no number is listed)

- BUSINESS PHONE LISTED (1 if a business telephone number is listed for the record, 0 if no number is listed)

- E-MAIL LISTED (1 if any e-mail address is listed for the record, 0 if no e-mail address of any kind is listed)

- MARITAL SINGLE OR MARITAL MISSING (1 if the record is listed as "single" or has no code at all listed in your marital status field, 0 if the record has any other code listed in your marital status field)

- PREFERRED YEAR OF GRADUATION (this should be a Y2K compliant year for whichever graduating class you associate the record with)

- LIFETIME GIVING (the total number of dollars this person has given to your institution since he or she has been in your database).

Once this file has been created, use Excel (or a statistics software package if you have one and can use it) to identify the oldest and youngest 25 percent of alumni by preferred year of graduation. Create two more fields in the Excel file: OLDEST 25% and YOUNGEST 25%. In each field assign a 1 to all records that belong to that quartile and a 0 to all the other records.

Here's the basic formula you can use to combine these fields into a score for each record in your Excel file:

SCORE = HOME PHONE LISTED(0/1) + BUSINESS PHONE LISTED(0/1) + E-MAIL LISTED(0/1) + OLDEST GRAD CLASS QUARTILE(0/1) – YOUNGEST GRAD CLASS QUARTILE(0/1) – MARITAL CODE SINGLE(0/1) – MARITAL CODE MISSING(0/1) + 3

(The constant of 3 at the end is a way to avoid negative and zero scores that can be confusing.)

It does look a little daunting. But it really isn't. Here are some data from a school that you can use to see if you understand the formula and how it works. Notice that I've provided the score for the first two records in this data set but have left the score for the last three records blank. Let's work through how the score was computed for these first two records. Then you can compute the score for the other three to make sure you understand.

ID	Home phone listed	Bus. phone listed	E-mail listed	1969 and earlier	1994 and later (–)	Marital missing (–)	Marital single (–)	Score (total +3)
1018	0	0	0	0	1	0	1	1
1019	1	0	1	0	1	0	1	3
1020	0	0	0	0	1	0	0	
1021	1	0	0	0	0	0	0	
1022	1	0	0	1	0	0	0	

We'll start with the first record, ID #1018. Notice that this person graduated in the youngest 25 percent (1994 and later) and is listed as single in the marital status field. Our formula says that record should get a –1 and another –1, making –2. But then we have to add a 3 on to that, for a score of 1.

Now let's do record #1019. This person has both a home phone listed and an e-mail listed making for a +2, but he or she also is in the youngest class quartile and is listed as single, making –2. So the +2 and the –2 cancel to 0, and then we add 3, to get a score of 3 for that person.

Now see if you can come up with a score for records #1020, #1021, and #1022. Then compare your answers with the data below:

ID	Home phone listed	Bus. phone listed	E-mail listed	1969 and earlier	1994 and later (–)	Marital missing (–)	Marital single (–)	Score (total +3)
1018	0	0	0	0	1	0	1	1
1019	1	0	1	0	1	0	1	3
1020	0	0	0	0	1	0	0	2
1021	1	0	0	0	0	0	0	4
1022	1	0	0	1	0	0	0	5

Once you understand how the score works, you can do the next two steps:

1. Add these 0/1 variables together using the formula to create a score for each of the 10,000 records in your file.

2. Compute the mean (average) lifetime dollars received from alumni at each score level.

If you need a little assistance to do these two steps, some math or statistics student or professor in your school should be able to help you.

How this score works for 10 different institutions

Earlier I mentioned that over the years I've foraged through a lot of alumni databases for good predictors of giving. In this section, I've laid out how the score you've just been looking at works for 10 schools that are representative of the more than 100 institutions I've studied. In a moment, I'd like you to browse through the data to see how remarkably well the score works for these schools—schools that differ greatly in terms of geographic location, size, money raised, whether they are public or private, and so on. But first let's go over the data for School 1 to make sure you understand what I've done in these tables. Going from left to right, here's a description of what's in each column of Table 4.1:

- **Score.** This column simply lists the scores I computed for the school's random sample of alumni records. Here the scores go from 1 to 7.

- **Count.** The next column displays the exact number of records for each score level in the sample.

- **Sum total giving.** This column shows the sum of lifetime giving for records at each score level. For example, for this school there are 1,069 alumni at score level 1 who have given a combined lifetime total of $3,291 to the school. At score level 7 there are 1,483 alumni who have given a combined lifetime total of $23,686,400 to the school. (No, you didn't misread anything. This is a good example of how powerful this simple little score can be.)

- **Mean total giving.** This column shows the mean (the arithmetic average) of lifetime giving for the records at each score level. I arrived at that number by dividing the sum total giving by the count. For example, for the 1,069 alumni at score level 1, the mean level of lifetime giving is $3. For the 1,483 alumni at score level 7, the mean level of lifetime giving is $15,972.

Table 4.1. Score results for School 1

SCORE = HOME PHONE LISTED + BUSINESS PHONE LISTED + E-MAIL
LISTED + 1969 OR EARLIER – 1994 OR LATER – MARITAL SINGLE –
MARITAL MISSING OR UNKNOWN + 3

Score	Count	Sum total giving	Mean total giving	Median total giving	Maximum lifetime amount
1	1,069	$3,291	$3	–	$425
2	5,974	$2,907,250	$487	–	$2,724,200
3	10,068	$1,941,510	$193	–	$345,570
4	12,290	$7,657,680	$623	–	$1,061,890
5	13,116	$24,780,600	$1,889	$27	$903,859
6	7,501	$56,208,800	$7,494	$113	$14,526,200
7	1,483	$23,686,400	$15,972	$261	$9,605,500

- **Median total giving.** This column shows the median of lifetime giving for the records at each score level—that is, the amount above and below which half the alumni at that score level fall in terms of lifetime giving. It's important to note a couple of things about the median. One, in every single instance throughout these 10 tables, the median is less than the mean—usually a *lot* less. That's because the median is not affected by large donors who can pull the mean way up. Notice, for example, that at score level 7 the mean is $15,972, but the median is $261. That's because there is one person at this score level who has given more than $9 million to the school, and the mean reflects that. The second thing to note about the median is that, for some score levels, there is no number listed. That simply means that more than half of the alumni at that score level have given nothing to the school.

- **Maximum lifetime amount.** This column shows the largest lifetime amount a graduate at each score level has given the school.

Go ahead and browse through the tables for the remaining nine schools. You'll see the formula I used for each school. It's pretty much the same for all of them. The chief differences you'll notice are the years I used to define the oldest and youngest graduating year quartiles, the way I defined the missing marital codes, and whether I counted home and work e-mail listings separately.

Table 4.2. Score results for School 2

SCORE = HOME PHONE LISTED + BUSINESS PHONE LISTED + HOME
E-MAIL LISTED + WORK E-MAIL LISTED + 1962 OR EARLIER – 1991
OR LATER – MARITAL SINGLE – MARITAL UNKNOWN + 3

Score	Count	Sum total giving	Mean total giving	Median total giving	Maximum lifetime amount
1	646	$20,931	$32	–	$5,770
2	1,684	$140,937	$84	–	$13,700
3	2,428	$855,777	$352	$20	$151,065
4	3,061	$8,960,600	$2,927	$160	$1,958,140
5	3,872	$22,911,000	$5,917	$570	$1,572,620
6	2,296	$23,738,800	$10,339	$1,015	$2,020,940
7	520	$5,978,130	$11,496	$1,350	$1,284,210
8	34	$902,304	$26,538	$3,733	$481,550

Table 4.3. Score results for School 3

SCORE = HOME PHONE LISTED + BUSINESS PHONE LISTED + HOME
E-MAIL LISTED + BUSINESS E-MAIL LISTED + 1976 OR EARLIER –
1990 OR LATER – MARITAL SINGLE – MARITAL MISSING – MARITAL
UNKNOWN + 3

Score	Count	Sum total giving	Mean total giving	Median total giving	Maximum lifetime amount
1	2,053	$21,314	$10	–	$760
2	5,981	$154,049	$26	–	$21,500
3	5,701	$243,130	$43	–	$4,238
4	3,555	$367,552	$103	–	$27,258
5	1,302	$250,948	$193	–	$18,250
6	416	$318,775	$766	$20	$199,240
7	152	$505,127	$3,323	$43	$365,525
8	12	$46,665	$3,889	$163	$42,100

Table 4.4. Score results for School 4

SCORE = HOME PHONE LISTED + BUSINESS PHONE LISTED + E-MAIL
LISTED + 1974 OR EARLIER – 1993 OR LATER – MARITAL SINGLE –
MARITAL MISSING + 3

Score	Count	Sum total giving	Mean total giving	Median total giving	Maximum lifetime amount
1	114	$706	$6	–	$235
2	1,071	$6,466	$6	–	$1,000
3	2,682	$39,191	$15	–	$2,035
4	2,982	$91,911	$31	–	$4,670
5	2,118	$188,079	$89	–	$20,600
6	653	$1,408,500	$2,157	–	$1,211,510
7	77	$67,004	$870	$50	$41,210

Table 4.5. Score results for School 5

SCORE = HOME PHONE LISTED + BUSINESS PHONE LISTED + E-MAIL
LISTED + 1966 OR EARLIER – 1993 OR LATER – MARITAL SINGLE –
MARITAL MISSING + 3

Score	Count	Sum total giving	Mean total giving	Median total giving	Maximum lifetime amount
1	447	$2,588	$6	–	$352
2	1,451	$51,989	$36	–	$5,215
3	2,247	$241,718	$108	$3	$16,340
4	2,472	$1,387,380	$561	$92	$79,992
5	2,757	$6,820,120	$2,474	$322	$737,724
6	2,169	$10,745,900	$4,954	$610	$4,250,050
7	273	$1,895,070	$6,942	$1,155	$341,868

Table 4.6. Score results for School 6

SCORE = HOME PHONE LISTED + BUSINESS PHONE LISTED + E-MAIL
LISTED + 1980 OR EARLIER – 1998 OR LATER – MARITAL SINGLE –
MARITAL MISSING + 3

Score	Count	Sum total giving	Mean total giving	Median total giving	Maximum lifetime amount
1	600	$3,405	$6	–	$425
2	1,957	$19,265	$10	–	$3,000
3	2,108	$103,468	$49	–	$25,973
4	1,994	$200,829	$101	–	$16,505
5	1,931	$645,547	$334	$12	$31,975
6	1,112	$4,680,200	$4,209	$70	$2,180,360
7	298	$1,461,470	$4,904	$295	$465,415

Table 4.7. Score results for School 7

SCORE = HOME PHONE LISTED + BUSINESS PHONE LISTED + E-MAIL
LISTED + 1968 OR EARLIER – 1994 OR LATER – MARITAL SINGLE –
MARITAL MISSING + 3

Score	Count	Sum total giving	Mean total giving	Median total giving	Maximum lifetime amount
1	664	$3,577	$5	–	$1,102
2	2,125	$95,016	$45	–	$32,500
3	1,975	$1,796,250	$909	–	$633,651
4	917	$1,424,000	$1,553	$10	$765,804
5	582	$1,982,870	$3,407	$100	$951,381
6	167	$901,767	$5,400	$250	$135,485
7	15	$118,126	$7,875	$100	$95,969

Table 4.8. Score results for School 8

SCORE = HOME PHONE LISTED + BUSINESS PHONE LISTED + E-MAIL
LISTED + 1967 OR EARLIER – 1994 OR LATER – MARITAL SINGLE –
MARITAL MISSING + 3

Score	Count	Sum total giving	Mean total giving	Median total giving	Maximum lifetime amount
1	144	$370	$3	–	$255
2	912	$5,686	$6	–	$339
3	1,704	$97,005	$57	–	$7,210
4	2,580	$1,509,950	$585	$25	$519,932
5	3,198	$7,639,950	$2,389	$115	$3,382,280
6	1,222	$2,103,510	$1,721	$241	$563,206
7	156	$256,614	$1,645	$468	$31,901

Table 4.9. Score results for School 9

SCORE = HOME PHONE LISTED + BUSINESS PHONE LISTED + E-MAIL
LISTED + 1974 OR EARLIER – 1995 OR LATER – MARITAL SINGLE –
MARITAL UNKNOWN + 3

Score	Count	Sum total giving	Mean total giving	Median total giving	Maximum lifetime amount
1	522	$537	$1	–	$125
2	1,766	$11,392	$6	–	$3,535
3	1,973	$33,522	$17	–	$3,500
4	2,489	$117,030	$47	–	$3,465
5	2,357	$358,932	$152	$5	$35,096
6	851	$325,813	$383	$35	$64,540
7	42	$35,559	$847	$193	$11,830

Table 4.10. Score results for School 10

SCORE = HOME PHONE LISTED + BUSINESS PHONE LISTED + E-MAIL
LISTED + 1964 OR EARLIER – 1990 OR LATER – MARITAL SINGLE –
MARITAL MISSING + 3

Score	Count	Sum total giving	Mean total giving	Median total giving	Maximum lifetime amount
1	81	$1,655	$20	–	$270
2	256	$5,201	$20	–	$500
3	325	$44,825	$138	–	$6,388
4	422	$597,375	$1,416	$45	$318,025
5	612	$2,066,430	$3,377	$250	$357,419
6	544	$2,302,410	$4,232	$475	$524,125
7	65	$344,355	$5,298	$760	$106,730

Running your own test

I've shown these graphs to lots of people, either individually or in group presentations. The reactions I get seem to fall into two camps:

- "Whoa!! That's really something. This is good stuff!"

- (Said with sort of a bored tone and a hint of a yawn) "Yeah, I guess I'm not that surprised. When you add all that stuff together it makes sense that the people with the higher scores would be giving more."

If you're in the first group, great! I've made the sale, and you don't need more convincing. If you're in the second group, I'm not sure what to say. The problem is, I'm very close to this stuff. I believe in it passionately, and, like a lot of people who are on a bit of a crusade, I'm not particularly patient and helpful with the "unconverted."

The last thing you need from me is more exhortation. Maybe the thing to do is just think about it awhile and see what happens. Maybe you'll change your mind; maybe you won't. Another thing you can do is ask someone else (who hasn't been exposed to anything I've said or written about data mining) to take a look at what I've laid out here. Their take on it may be thought-provoking and helpful.

But for now I'll assume you're convinced this little score has some potential. I'll even assume you're willing to try it out at your own institution to see how it works and whether (limited as it is) it might help you quickly save money and make more on annual fund appeals.

If you are willing to try it out, here's what I'd recommend:

1. Create a list of alumni whom you plan to solicit by phone, mail, or e-mail over the next several months.

2. With the help of your IT staff, compute scores for these alumni, and get those scores into your database.

3. Go ahead and appeal to these alumni as if the scores didn't exist. That is, don't make any decisions about segmenting these alumni based on the scores. Just do what you would normally do as if you'd never read this article.

4. Once the appeal has ended, do some analysis by score level of what you received. For example, for each score level, compute the percentage of alumni who gave anything at all by check or credit card. Compute the percentage of alumni who made a pledge. Compute the mean and median dollars given by check or credit card. Compute the mean and median dollars pledged.

If you do all that, you'll learn a huge amount even if the results you get aren't as stellar as I expect they'll be. My expectations are much less important than your willingness to take on the role of applied scientist, and to test ideas, theories, and just plain hunches that may help you do a better job of achieving your institution's advancement mission. We need more of that in this business—a lot more.

PART III

Analyzing Donor Types

Chapter 5

Making Connections
with Online Givers

What's different about donors who give via the Web?

Originally published in 2004 on www.case.org

Author's note: *I wrote this paper in the spring of 2004 shortly after analyzing data from five higher-education institutions. As I read it and reread it almost four years later, I like the way it flows and I like the messages it conveys. But I'm also aware of how much the Web has changed since then. For example, pick up any book with a copyright date of 1997 or earlier. Maybe you can find one that has a company Web site listed in it. I can't (and I look at a lot of books). That's how new the Web is. Yet how it has changed all of our lives!*

So, the paper is kind of an antique. On the other hand, I have to admit disappointment at how slow schools have been to pick up on the tremendous power of the Web to help them raise money and to predict who will do the giving. For example, I think it should be easy for schools to assign "Web metrics" to alumni who are registered members of their online community. Metrics like number of e-mails opened, number of click-throughs to the Web site, average amount of time spent on the site, and so on. In the few instances where we've been able to look at the relationship between such metrics and giving at a school, the metrics work well as predictors. Alumni who open e-mails are better donors than those who don't. Alumni who click through to the site from an opened e-mail give more than those who don't. That's encouraging. What's not encouraging is how hard it is for schools to develop such metrics. It shouldn't be hard; it should be easy.

ONLINE GIVING. What a concept for any fundraising organization! Donors simply log on to your Web site and make their contributions. No headaches over production and format costs for mailers. No site visits for travel-weary development officers. No hiring callers for the phonathon. Far less likelihood of unfulfilled pledges. Wouldn't that be great?

We all know, of course, it's not that easy. Nonetheless, the notion of online giving is enormously intriguing, and it's here to stay. Something that was only an idea less than a decade ago has become a reality that is growing and changing so fast that what I've written here will be a little dated by the time you read it.

One of the many arenas where online giving has established a foothold is higher education. All colleges and universities now have sophisticated Web sites, and many of them have made it (fairly) easy for alumni and others (e.g., parents and friends) to make electronic donations. But who are these donors? How prevalent are they? How do they differ from the majority of donors who have never made an electronic gift? Do these online donors tend to be younger people who are more comfortable with computers and the Internet than more "mature" graduates who may still miss the rotary phone?

To begin to get answers to these kinds of questions, I launched a little study in the spring of 2004. Five four-year higher-education institutions ranging from small and private to large and public each sent me a random sample of about 10,000 records that included regular givers and nongivers but no online givers. Each institution also sent me records for all its online givers. The smallest group of online givers I got was slightly over 200 records; the largest was about 750. Clearly, online giving was in its infancy at these schools and (safe to assume) most academic institutions.

Each school sent me these fields:

- lifetime giving,

- online giving (for relevant records),

- home phone listed (Y/N),

- business phone listed (Y/N),

- e-mail listed (Y/N),

- preferred year of graduation, and

- marital status.

As you might imagine, I was able to do a lot of analyses with these data. But what I've done in this article is hit some of the high points, specifically:

- how online givers compare with regular givers,

- how class year relates to lifetime giving for online givers,

- how marital status relates to lifetime giving for online givers, and

- how to use a simple score to identify major giving prospects among online givers.

How online givers compare with regular givers

Throughout the analysis, I largely ignored the amounts people had given online. I was more interested in the amounts online givers had given over their lifetimes. And what I expected to find was a younger crowd who was comfortable with the Internet and computers and who had made relatively small gifts as first-time donors.

That's not what I found. Yes, it's a younger crowd, insofar as more of them are young than old. But, as Table 5.1 shows, the median level of lifetime giving was much greater for these online givers than for regular givers, without exception across the five schools. For example, in School C, where the difference between online and regular givers was the least, the median for online givers was still 50 percent higher than the median for regular givers.

How class year relates to lifetime giving for online givers

Although many university advancement offices are unaware of it, there is a powerful relationship between how long alumni have been out of school and how much they have given to their alma maters. For example, Table 5.2 shows the median lifetime giving for regular donors across the five schools by class-year quartile.

Table 5.1. Median lifetime giving dollars for regular givers and online givers across five schools

	Regular givers	Online givers
School A	$485	$1,105
School B	$115	$654
School C	$213	$325
School D	$241	$390
School E	$405	$925

Table 5.2. Median lifetime giving dollars for regular givers by class-year quartile

	1st quartile (oldest 25% of alumni)	2nd quartile	3rd quartile	4th quartile (youngest 25% of alumni)
School A	$1,095	$708	$350	$100
School B	$205	$137	$75	$50
School C	$760	$300	$189	$55
School D	$670	$300	$145	$40
School E	$1,300	$710	$320	$100

Table 5.3. Median lifetime giving dollars for online givers by class-year quartile

	1st quartile (oldest 25% of alumni)	2nd quartile	3rd quartile	4th quartile (youngest 25% of alumni)
School A	$2,801	$2,080	$1,282	$280
School B	$1,073	$620	$340	$110
School C	$1,170	$355	$340	$125
School D	$1,643	$985	$397	$83
School E	$2,728	$1,680	$1,237	$325

If you compare the medians for the oldest 25 percent of alumni against the medians for the youngest 25 percent, it's easy to see that the oldest group has given at least four times as much as the youngest group (School B) and (more typically) at least 10 times as much.

Table 5.3 shows the same lifetime medians for online givers. Notice that the relative differences between the oldest and youngest quartiles are about the same as for the regular givers. That is, the oldest alumni have given about 10 or more times as much as the youngest alumni. So the pronounced overall difference in lifetime giving rates by age group appears to hold up for online givers as well as regular givers.

How marital status relates to lifetime giving for online givers

Among the 70 or so college and university donor databases I've looked at over the last five years, there has almost always been a strong relationship between the codes in the "marital status" field and lifetime giving. Specifically, alumni listed as "single" or "missing" within this field give less, and less frequently, than alumni with any other kind of code.

With the data for this study, I was not able to clearly classify records across the five schools into "single" and "missing." However, I was able to divide alumni into those listed as "married" versus those listed with any other code (including missing data).

Tables 5.4 and 5.5 show the median lifetime giving for "marrieds" versus all other marital codes for both regular and online givers for each of the five schools. From Table 5.4, you'll see that, for regular givers, the "marrieds" give considerably more than the other marital codes (without exception) across the five schools. I expected this result.

Table 5.4. Median lifetime giving dollars for regular givers by marital status

	Married	All other codes
School A	$685	$225
School B	$170	$64
School C	$300	$100
School D	$203	$100
School E	$775	$130

Table 5.5. Median lifetime giving dollars for online givers by marital status

	Married	All other codes
School A	$1,420	$580
School B	$514	$219
School C	$348	$200
School D	$880	$175
School E	$1,425	$325

However, I didn't know what to expect with online givers. As you can see from Table 5.5, it turns out that married online givers also give considerably more than online givers with other marital codes.

How to use a simple score to identify major giving prospects among online givers

I spend most of my professional time teaching university and nonprofit development staff how to do data mining on their own databases. Many staff members are prospect researchers who, of course, have a keen interest in major giving. So, at the end of this study, I put my teaching hat on and asked myself: "Let's say I were using the limited data in this project to help prospect researchers identify major giving prospects among online givers. Is there a simple score I could construct that might help them pick out good prospects?" (For more information on this process, see Chapter 4, "A Simple Score.")

To answer the question, I developed this scoring formula for each school:

SCORE = MARRIED(0/1) + OLDEST-GRAD CLASS QUARTILE(0/1) – YOUNGEST-GRAD CLASS QUARTILE(0/1) + 2

If this looks a little confusing, let me clarify. Each record received a score calculated from the following components:

■ If the marital status field said "married," it got a 1; otherwise a 0.

■ If it was in the oldest-grad quartile, it got a 1; otherwise a 0.

■ If it was in the youngest-grad quartile, it got a *minus* 1; otherwise a 0.

Table 5.6. Median lifetime giving dollars for online givers by score level

	Score			
	1	**2**	**3**	**4**
School A	$210	$935	$1,555	$4,254
School B	$70	$300	$500	$1,150
School C	$125	$230	$334	$1,323
School D	$55	$313	$985	$1,755
School E	$230	$475	$1,695	$3,652

I added a constant of "2" at the end of the formula to ensure that there would be no negative or zero scores. All scores at each school ranged from 1 to 4. Table 5.6 shows the median lifetime giving of online givers for each score level for each school.

Interesting. At each school, the level of lifetime giving goes up dramatically with score level. But how could a prospect researcher use these scores to help a gift officer (someone who actually calls on major giving prospects) find new potential donors?

Let's work through a little example. At right is a list from one of the schools of 21 online alumni givers who received a score of 4. For each record, a letter ID is listed along with the lifetime amounts (altered to completely protect the identity of the school) donated by the person.

Putting myself in the shoes of the prospect researcher, these are some of the thoughts I might have about this list:

- I'm certain that graduate "G," who has donated almost a million dollars to the school, is already on some gift officer's radar screen. (We're in big trouble if I'm wrong.)

- With some misgivings, I'll make the same assumption about graduate "H," who has donated over $40,000.

- For the rest of them (that is, the remaining 19 alumni), I would sit down with at least one gift officer and say, "How about if we take a closer look at these folks? Let's see what their contact history is. For those who haven't been contacted, let's call them up or write them a personalized letter. I think it may lead to something very good."

ID	Life Giving
G	$984,991
H	$40,978
M	$18,358
C	$8,434
I	$8,245
D	$5,956
P	$4,676
J	$4,671
R	$3,703
N	$3,643
E	$3,263
T	$2,220
S	$2,148
L	$2,128
F	$1,553
U	$825
Q	$790
O	$615
B	$614
A	$537
K	$77

Closing thoughts

Clearly, this limited study only begins to scratch the surface of online giving and its future in university fundraising. And, of course, it doesn't even touch on the enormous potential for this method of raising money for nonprofits.

But the results I've presented here show the importance of doing something we so very often do not do in development: analyze data that can provide us with important answers as to who our donors are and how best to appeal to them. We all have opinions about donor behavior. And some of us express those opinions so authoritatively and convincingly that our colleagues run the risk of accepting them as fundamental principles, as axioms.

Well, opinions are fine. But if we don't test those opinions with data—data that are now very accessible—we end up being pontificators rather than applied scientists willing to follow where the data take us. I think we have legions of young people in our profession who are champing at the bit to do this kind of science. We need to train them and then cut them loose on the data. If we do that, I have every conviction they will bring back answers we never dreamed of. And those answers will allow us to do great good for great causes.

Chapter 6

Greeks Bearing Gifts

*Understanding fraternity and sorority graduates . . .
and other alumni groups*

Originally published in 2007 on www.case.org

Author's note: *I wrote this one in 2007, shortly before the publication of this book. There's nothing earth-shattering about it. Bottom line, it says that if your institution has Greek organizations (and if they've been around a while), the alumni who belonged to those organizations (a) are more likely than their classmates to have given you something, and (b) have probably given gifts that are, on average, larger than those of their classmates. Maybe that seems obvious. But of the many schools I've seen that have (or have had) Greek organizations, the great majority have never looked to see whether the formerly Greek alumni are or are not better givers. Nor have they used that information to do a more effective job of raising money. And the same can be said for other information like reunion attendance, volunteer activity, being a member of the online community, and a host of other variables that are highly related to giving. That's not a good thing.*

THE INJUNCTION "Beware of Greeks bearing gifts" refers to the gift of the Trojan horse and the calamity it brought. I have to admit I didn't know the origin of the phrase until I recently looked it up—another reminder of how the great works were wasted on me in my teens and early 20s. But I'd like to draw your attention to a different kind of Greeks bearing altogether different gifts.

Hardly a business day goes by that I don't exhort advancement professionals to pay attention to how the vast amount of information they store on alumni can point to people who are likely to give frequently and give a lot. If I've talked to you, or if you've read some of what I've written, you may be saying or thinking, "Peter, I think we got that by now."

But if you haven't been worn out by my refrain, let me offer yet another piece of evidence that certain data about your alumni may help you identify those among them who are more likely to contribute to your institution. That piece of data, of course, is whether someone had a Greek affiliation—that is, was a member of a fraternity or sorority—while an undergraduate at your school.

I'd like to show you some graphs that I think tell a compelling story about the difference in giving across a 50-year span for Greeks and non-Greeks at six different higher-education institutions. I hope you will end up agreeing with me that the story is compelling. But there's something more important I'm hoping for—because you may not have (or have ever had) Greek organizations at your school. This comes back to my usual refrain: I'm hoping you will agree that foraging through your alumni database to find new predictors of giving is worth the effort. Because not doing that kind of foraging and not taking advantage of those predictors in your appeals and campaigns is leaving the generosity of many of your alumni untapped. And that's not a good thing.

In this article, I'll talk about:

- the data I used,

- what I uncovered, and

- some implications for what I found.

The data I used

All the data I used came from six four-year higher-education institutions spread around the country. Five of them were private universities; one was a large public institution. For the smaller schools, I used records of all the solicitable alumni in their databases. For the larger ones, I used a random sample of at least 10,000 records. The specific variables I used for the project included these:

- whether a person was listed in the database as having belonged to a Greek organization as an undergraduate,

- the preferred year of graduation for each person, and

- the total lifetime giving of each person at the time I gathered the data.

For each of the six schools I studied, I wanted to answer these four questions:

1. Was there a difference in the rate of lifetime giving between Greeks and non-Greeks?

2. How did the rates of giving for Greeks and non-Greeks change as a function of the length of time these people had been out of school?

3. For those Greeks and non-Greeks who had ever given anything to their schools, was there a difference in the median lifetime giving between the two groups?

4. If so, how did this difference in the median lifetime giving between Greeks and non-Greeks change as a function of how long they had been out of school?

What I uncovered

To answer the first two questions, I computed the percentage of Greeks and non-Greeks who had ever given anything to their schools at each of 11 five-year intervals since year of graduation (e.g., 5 years or less, 6–10 years, 11–15 years, etc., on out to 50 years or more). The results for School A appear in Figure 6.1. Notice the very large differences in lifetime giving rates between Greeks and non-Greeks regardless of how long the alumni had been out of school. In fact, the lifetime giving rates of non-Greeks who were out more than 20 years seemed to drop off a bit, while those for Greeks stayed about the same.

Figure 6.1. Lifetime donor participation rates by Greeks and non-Greeks since graduation for School A

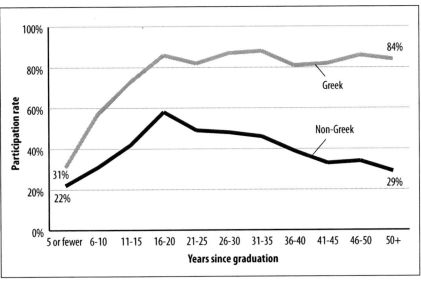

Figure 6.2. Lifetime donor participation rates by Greeks and non-Greeks since graduation for School B

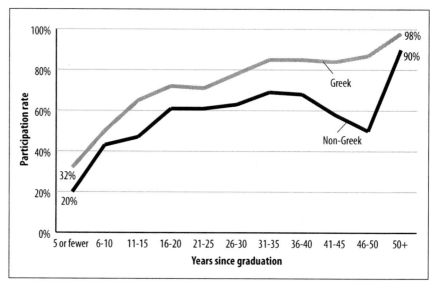

Figure 6.3. Lifetime donor participation rates by Greeks and non-Greeks since graduation for School C

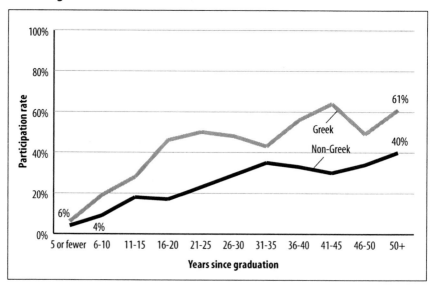

Figure 6.4. Lifetime donor participation rates by Greeks and non-Greeks since graduation for School D

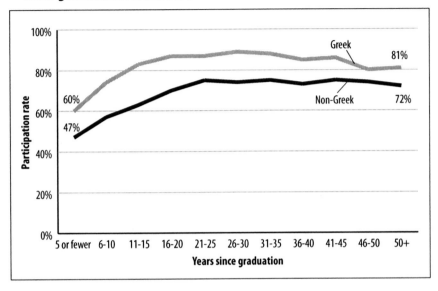

Figure 6.5. Lifetime donor participation rates by Greeks and non-Greeks since graduation for School E

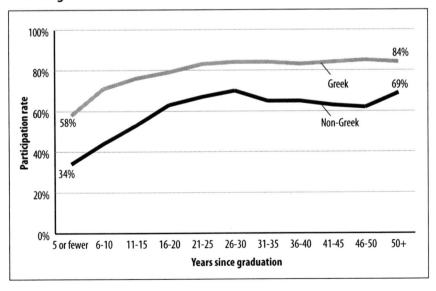

Figure 6.6. Lifetime donor participation rates by Greeks and non-Greeks since graduation for School F

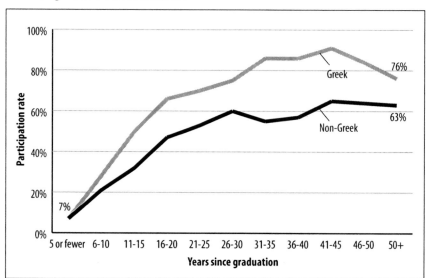

But that's just one institution—School A. Take a look at the graphs for the remaining schools (Figures 6.2 through 6.6). Then let's go back to the first two questions I was trying to answer:

1. Was there a difference in the rate of lifetime giving between Greeks and non-Greeks?

2. How did the rates of giving for Greeks and non-Greeks change as a function of the length of time these people had been out of school?

For the first question, I think the answer is unequivocal. In *none* of the schools did the lifetime participation rates of non-Greeks *ever* exceed those of the Greeks. In fact, in only one instance (alumni at School E who had been out of school five years or less) were the participation rates the same. When I saw this pattern unfold, I knew I had to write this article.

But how about the second question? Here I think it's harder to give a general response. About the best I can do is to say that the difference in lifetime participation between Greeks and non-Greeks typically seemed to widen as the time since graduation increased—but not always. Sometimes the gap between the two groups narrowed. Still, the Greeks were always ahead.

Now consider questions three and four:

3. For those Greeks and non-Greeks who had ever given anything to their schools, was there a difference in the median lifetime giving between the two groups?

4. If so, how did this difference in the median lifetime giving between Greeks and non-Greeks change as a function of how long they had been out of school?

To answer these questions, I looked at the median lifetime giving by age group for Greeks and non-Greeks for *only* those alumni who had ever made a gift. We've seen that the Greeks were consistently better participators, but what about the actual amount of the gifts the two groups were making?

Let's turn now to the next six graphs (Figures 6.7 through 6.12). Data can be whimsical; they just don't always give us the definitive answers we'd like. But here's what I see in these graphs: In general, the Greeks gave more than the non-Greeks, and that difference tended to widen the longer the alumni were out of school.

To summarize an answer to all four questions, I'd say the Greeks were definitely better participators than the non-Greeks; their gifts tended to be larger than those of the non-Greeks; and the older Greeks generally gave more than the older non-Greeks.

Figure 6.7. Median lifetime giving by Greeks and non-Greeks by years since graduation for School A

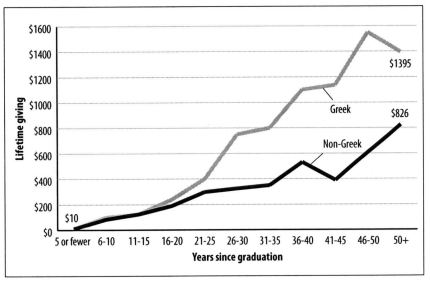

Figure 6.8. Median lifetime giving by Greeks and non-Greeks by years since graduation for School B

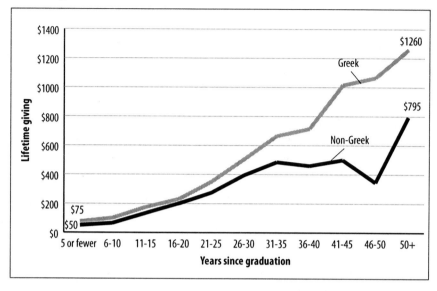

Figure 6.9. Median lifetime giving by Greeks and non-Greeks by years since graduation for School C

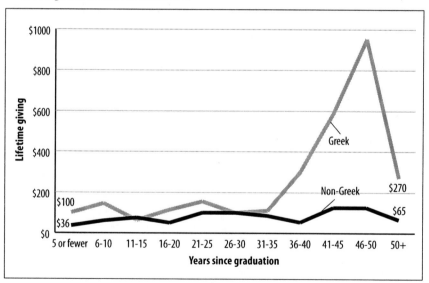

Figure 6.10. Median lifetime giving by Greeks and non-Greeks by years since graduation for School D

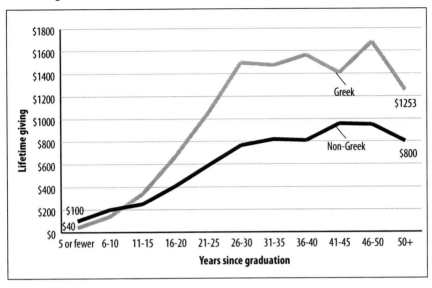

Figure 6.11. Median lifetime giving by Greeks and non-Greeks by years since graduation for School E

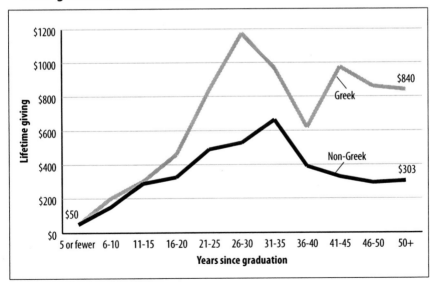

Figure 6.12. Median lifetime giving by Greeks and non-Greeks by years since graduation for School F

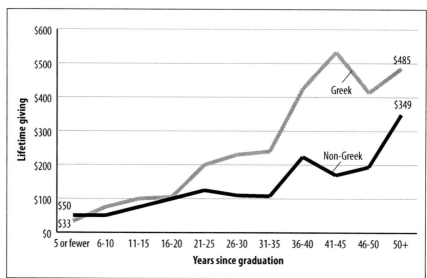

Implications

I think there are several points to take away from all of this:

- First of all, if you've read this far, you're already thinking about the possible usefulness to your own institution of what I've reported. You're coming up with ideas I've never considered. That's good.

- If you have (or have had) alumni in your database who are listed as belonging to a Greek organization while undergraduates, look at what your data reveal. (Don't worry too much about how the data got in there. On a record-by-record basis, your IT people won't know.) Do the students in your call center have more luck getting pledges from Greeks versus non-Greeks? How about with snail-mail appeals? How about with major campaigns?

- Most importantly, start pushing to uncover other kinds of data you have that can help predict who's going to give and give a lot. For example, do you keep track of reunion attendance? If you do, look at the difference between Greeks who've attended at least two reunions and all other alumni. I think you'll be amazed at what good givers these folks can be.

PART IV

Managing Fundraising Activity

Chapter 7

Baseball, Fundraising, and the 80/20 Rule

What proportion of donors is responsible for the most giving?

Originally published in 2005 on www.case.org

Author's note: *I wrote this piece in the fall of 2004. Unlike the paper about online giving (Chapter 5), I think this one is still very timely. As you read through the beginning of the paper, you'll see why I included "baseball" and "the 80/20 rule" in the title. The thrust of the paper is this: Any way you look at the numbers, it's clear that a very small percentage of alumni accounts for a hugely disproportionate amount of the giving in higher education. There's a good chance you suspected this; here you can see your suspicions confirmed with hard data.*

EVER SINCE I HEARD ABOUT the 80/20 rule, back in the mid-'70s, I've been intrigued by it. The rule emerged almost a hundred years ago from the work of Italian economist Vilfredo Pareto, who observed that 80 percent of the wealth in Italy was owned by 20 percent of the country's families. Pareto, an avid gardener, also noticed his wealth theory applied to plant productivity—20 percent of his peapods seemed to account for 80 percent of the peas he harvested.

For most of my professional life I've been applying the 80/20 rule to time management. Just about every day I make up a list of things to do. The list usually contains 10 items. I figure if I can complete the two most important items on the list, I'll get 80 percent of the value I'd get from completing all 10. It's been a good system for me. Maybe the only kink is that Linda, my wife of almost 30 years, doesn't always agree with the two items I choose.

When I first started doing data mining in the fundraising arena, I thought the 80/20 rule might well apply there. It made sense to me that about 80 percent of the money raised from any given database would have been contributed by about 20 percent of the records in that database. But I never got around to systematically checking out my hunch until the fall of 2004, after I picked up an obscure but fascinating book that inspired me to perform some analyses that fueled the writing of this article.

We'll get back to that book shortly. At this point, though, you may be wondering about the word "baseball" in the title of this article. I'll be honest. I love the data-analysis work I do. It fascinates me. But it doesn't fascinate everybody. In fact, it bores or confuses more people than it fascinates. I threw in the baseball idea as a way to get more people to read this piece, and to make the project more interesting for me, too.

Hits and home runs

Let's start with the baseball. How does the 80/20 rule apply to data that are routinely reported in the sports section of your newspaper during the major-league baseball season?

Thanks to the Internet, you can find information with a click of a mouse that only a few years ago would have taken weeks of drudgery to uncover. I didn't have much trouble finding a Web site that reported batting data for major-league ballplayers who had a minimum of 370 at-bats for the 2004 regular season. There were 154 players in this group. I chose two categories to look at: hits and home runs.

How does the 80/20 rule apply to hits? In Table 7.1, you can see that the top 20 percent of hit-producing batters had a total of 5,920 hits; the bottom 80 percent of hit producers had a total of 17,996 hits. It doesn't look like the 80/20 rule is working here. The last column in the table shows that the top 20 percent of hit producers produced 25 percent of the total hits for the entire group of 154 batters—just a bit more than their fair share. If the 80/20 rule were working, we'd expect these players to have produced about 19,000 hits, not the 5,920 hits they did produce.

Table 7.1. Number of hits and percentage of hits by top 20% and bottom 80% of hit producers

Player group	Number of players	Number of hits	Percentage of total hits
Top 20%	31	5,920	25%
Bottom 80%	123	17,996	75%
Total	154	23,916	100%

Table 7.2. Number of home runs and percentage of home runs by top 20% and bottom 80% of home-run producers

Player group	Number of players	Number of home runs	Percentage of total home runs
Top 20%	30	1,111	35%
Bottom 80%	124	2,090	65%
Total	154	3,201	100%

How does the 80/20 rule apply to home runs? In Table 7.2, you can see that the rule doesn't seem to be working here either. The last column in the table shows that the top 20 percent of home-run producers hit 35 percent of the total home runs among the entire group of 154 batters. That's certainly more than their fair share, but if the 80/20 rule were working, we'd expect this group to have hit about 2,560 home runs, not the 1,111 they did hit.

Elite donors and other donors

Now let's talk about fundraising. Earlier I said I had never gotten around to systematically checking out my initial hunch that about 80 percent of the money raised from any given database would have been contributed by about 20 percent of the records in that database. But although I had never "systematically" examined this, just from eyeballing a lot of data over the years I knew—just as you probably know already—that the 80/20 rule didn't apply. In this case, however, the 80/20 rule is far too conservative. In most databases, the top 20 percent of donors usually account for over 95 percent of total dollars contributed.

Then, as I mentioned above, I bought a book called *Psychology, Science, and History: An Introduction to Historiometry*, written in 1990 by Dean Keith Simonton, a psychology professor at University of California, Davis. I found it interesting but definitely not something I'd recommend to the casual reader. (After I sent an e-mail to Professor Simonton, in which I extolled the book, he replied that it had not achieved commercial success: "Too technical.")

Halfway through the book, Simonton begins talking about the productivity of scientists, and he mentions something called the "Price law," based on D.L. Price's 1963 book *Little Science, Big Science*. Simonton writes, "According to the Price law, if k represents the total number of contributors to a discipline, then the square root of k will be the predicted number of contributors who generate half of all contributions."

That's very different from the 80/20 rule. If the Price law applies to fundraising databases—or, more particularly, alumni databases—that means that a *very* small proportion of all the records are accounting for a huge, huge amount of the giving. In fact, as the size of the database increases, the percentage of total records that accounts for half of the contributions *decreases*.

For example, look at Table 7.3. Suppose your alumni database contains 10,000 records. That means, according to the Price law, that about 100 alumni (1 percent of your database) account for at least 50 percent of the total dollars that have been donated by all the alumni. But let's say you have 100,000 alumni in your database. The square root of 100,000 is about 316. And 316 is only a third of a percent of 100,000.

Could it be that such a very small proportion of alumni really contribute such a disproportionate amount to their alma maters? To begin to answer this question, I took two basic steps:

1. I pulled together random samples of alumni databases from five different four-year institutions that differed markedly from one another in terms of public versus private affiliation, geographic location, and size. All of the samples were between 10,000 and 55,000 records. The only variables included in each of these samples were "preferred year of graduation" and "lifetime giving." (To protect the confidentiality of each institution, I did a currency conversion so that the dollar values are not the actual amounts. However, all percentages reported are exactly the same as for the original dollar amounts.)

2. For each sample, I computed the square root of the number of records in the sample. For example, one of the samples contained exactly 10,000 records; the square root for that sample, then, was 100. I then identified that same number

Table 7.3. Square roots and relative percentages of four different-sized hypothetical databases

# of solicitable records	Square root of solicitable records	Square root as percentage of # of solicitable records
1,000	32	3.2%
10,000	100	1.0%
100,000	316	0.3%
500,000	707	0.1%

Table 7.4. Total lifetime giving and corresponding percentages for top group of alumni donors and all others at School A

Group	Count	Total lifetime giving	Percentage of total lifetime giving
Top group	232	$142,118,390	77%
All others	53,430	$41,653,716	23%
Total	53,662	$183,772,100	100%

of top donors (with this example, then, the top 100 lifetime donors). I computed the total lifetime giving for this top group of donors and then computed the percentage that amount represented of the total lifetime giving for the entire sample.

The results appear in Tables 7.4 through 7.8. We'll consider Table 7.4 in detail as an example. Notice that the total number of records shown for School A in Table 7.4 is 53,662. The square root of this number is 232 (actually, a fraction less than that). These top 232 alumni contributed a total of $142,118,390. That's about 77 percent of the total of $183,772,100 contributed by all the records in the sample.

Surprisingly (to me anyway), Table 7.4 shows that the Price law *underestimates* the giving of this elite group of alumni donors. According to the Price law, this group should have contributed about $91,500,000, or half of the total of $183,772,100.

The same pattern holds in the remaining tables (7.5–7.8). In each of the four other schools, the Price law underestimates the giving of the elite group:

■ In School B (Table 7.5) the elite group (101 alumni) accounts for 83 percent of the $34,272,637 contributed by all the records in the sample.

■ In School C (Table 7.6) the elite group (106 alumni) accounts for 81 percent of the $38,448,600 contributed by all the records in the sample.

■ In School D (Table 7.7) the elite group (101 alumni) accounts for 68 percent of the $35,265,042 contributed by all the records in the sample.

■ In School E (Table 7.8) the elite group (134 alumni) accounts for 60 percent of the $61,233,355 contributed by all the records in the sample.

To me these data are astounding. Any way you look at the numbers, it's clear that a *very* small proportion of alumni accounts for a hugely disproportionate

Table 7.5. Total lifetime giving and corresponding percentages for top group of alumni donors and all others at School B

Group	Count	Total lifetime giving	Percentage of total lifetime giving
Top group	101	$28,556,805	83%
All others	9,899	$5,715,832	17%
Total	10,000	$34,272,637	100%

Table 7.6. Total lifetime giving and corresponding percentages for top group of alumni donors and all others at School C

Group	Count	Total lifetime giving	Percentage of total lifetime giving
Top group	106	$31,319,700	81%
All others	11,118	$7,128,900	19%
Total	11,224	$38,448,600	100%

Table 7.7. Total lifetime giving and corresponding percentages for top group of alumni donors and all others at School D

Group	Count	Total lifetime giving	Percentage of total lifetime giving
Top group	101	$24,103,802	68%
All others	10,199	$11,161,241	32%
Total	10,300	$35,265,042	100%

Table 7.8. Total lifetime giving and corresponding percentages for top group of alumni donors and all others at School E

Group	Count	Total lifetime giving	Percentage of total lifetime giving
Top group	134	$36,528,184	60%
All others	17,747	$24,705,171	40%
Total	17,881	$61,233,355	100%

amount of the giving. And given the variety of schools included in this study, there is plenty of reason to assume this phenomenon exists throughout higher education—at least until someone comes along and provides convincing data to the contrary.

But for me the question becomes, "What do we do about this?" I'd like to divide my closing remarks between two topics: what I think we're already doing, and one other thing I'd like to see us do as soon as possible.

What we're already doing

If "we" means all the thousands of professionals who work in the arena of higher-education advancement, I'd say we're doing three things pretty well: stewardship, prospect research, and predictive modeling.

Stewardship. Stewardship is far away from my primary area of expertise (data mining). Nonetheless, I have the strong impression that the people in charge of major giving at schools are doing a reasonably conscientious job of taking care of and nurturing the kinds of elite major donors shown in Tables 7.4–7.8. Gift officers and vice presidents and even presidents call on these "heavy hitters" frequently to keep them happy and involved in the ongoing campaigns of the schools they so generously support. They get the box seats at the football games. They get buildings and endowed chairs and professional schools named after them. They get on the boards of trustees. In short, these donors are treated far better than the "ultra customers" in the private sector who get the flight upgrades, free nights at luxury hotels, and other perquisites.

Prospect research. I'm not an expert in prospect research, either, but I know much more about it than I do about stewardship. Simply put, I think the goal of prospect research has always been to uncover individuals who are not yet (but can become) the elite donors we're talking about here.

At least two things in higher-education prospect research are noteworthy:

- The creation of a distinct profession within advancement. Over the last 30-or-so years, prospect research has come into its own as a profession within fundraising in general and higher education in particular. When someone says, "I'm a prospect researcher, and I belong to APRA," we all know what that means (the Association of Professional Researchers for Advancement). These people are dedicated professionals eager to improve their skills and help development officers approach people of means for major gifts.

- The increasing scope and accuracy of screening data. With the advent of the Internet and galloping computer technology, the quality of screening data available to schools and nonprofits at reasonable prices is getting better and better. Gone forever are the days of searching through cumbersome directories that were obsolete the moment they were printed.

Predictive modeling. Predictive modeling is still a new kid on the block in advancement, but that situation is changing rapidly. Of that I'm certain, because about all I do professionally is teach advancement professionals how to do predictive modeling.

What's particularly exciting is that not only are more schools getting interested in tapping their databases for good predictors of giving, but also that the Web is coming of age. It's now possible to capture specific behavioral data in a Web log (number of visits to the site, length of time per visit, what pages were accessed, etc.). I call these data "Web metrics." The creation of these metrics puts us on the verge of doing a much better job of identifying who the future givers—especially major givers—are likely to be.

What we should do now

About 80 percent of the elite donors identified in Tables 7.4–7.8 belong to the oldest 25 percent of alumni in each of the five schools. Practically speaking, this usually means people who have been out of school about 30 years or more.

In addition to knowing that these donors are over 50, what else can we say about them? From my own work, I know a few things that separate them from their peers:

- They're much more likely to have attended at least one reunion since graduation.

- They're much more likely to have a spouse or other family member listed in the database.

- They're much more likely to have given a gift online.

- They're much more likely to have participated as a volunteer after graduating.

While this kind of information is useful from a predictive standpoint, it's meager from the standpoint of finding out who they really are and why they've been so generous to their alma maters. It's time to change that. It's time we start doing research of a careful scientific nature that can only be done by established research organizations (the University of Michigan Survey Research Center is a good example) that have the expertise to conduct in-depth interviewing of these elite donors (along with samples of their peers who have given their schools little or nothing).

Such research is not inexpensive. But there are foundations and government agencies that would support it if effectively approached. Let's get the ball rolling. The value to our field could be enormous.

Chapter 8

What Makes a Phone Call Successful?

A case for analyzing call-center data

Originally published in 2006 on www.case.org

Author's note: *I wrote this paper in 2006 after doing an exploratory study in an area crying out for comprehensive research. What I reported in the paper may not hold up when studies are done at other schools with better variables and better experimental designs than I used. That said, I think I uncovered three factors that appear strongly related to whether a given call yields a pledge, the size of the pledge, and whether the caller is able to get a credit card payment for the pledge: who is called, the experience of the caller, and how long the call lasts.*

Still, although the data here show a statistical relationship between these factors and giving, we don't know whether these factors actually cause the better results. Without further research, for instance, we can't tell whether having callers stay on the phone longer will improve success. But with luck, this article will at least stimulate your thinking. If you come up with alternative explanations about why the relationships exist, that's fine. And if this article gets somebody to actually do some controlled research on the problem, that would be really good!

I'VE BEEN DOING DATA MINING in fundraising for the better part of nine years now, and the lion's share of my efforts has been in educational advancement. If you've read some of the articles I've written, you know I'm always pushing institutions to analyze the huge amount of information they collect on their alumni. My point (repetitious and tiresome as it might be) is simple: If you don't analyze this data, you're ignoring powerful predictors of giving. Put more bluntly, you're leaving money on the table for some other worthy (or not so worthy) cause to come along and scoop up.

For a number of years I've been thinking about all the calling that educational institutions do. Some call hundreds of thousands of alumni in a year's time. Recently I've started educating myself about all the data that colleges, universities, and schools collect and store electronically regarding what happens in these calls. If you're even tangentially involved with the work of your call center, you know that a huge amount of data get stored. A few examples:

- time, date, and duration of call,

- caller gender,

- city, state, and zip code of graduate,

- result of call (call back, pledge, refusal, etc.),

- birth date of graduate, and

- whether the graduate works for an organization that will match a gift.

And on and on it goes. But here's the rub: I don't see much evidence that all these data are getting effectively analyzed—analyzed so these institutions can maximize the huge amount of time, cost, and energy they put into their calling programs.

We could speculate on some reasons for this lack of analysis, but right now I just want to fire you up. I want to take you through a mini investigation of some data I analyzed at a university that does an enormous of amount of calling. I hope what I say will intrigue you and cause you to conclude that you need to be doing this kind of analysis on your own calling data.

Some background

The university that provided the data for this study is a large institution with a very active call center. Calls are made five days a week by a staff of 30-or-so student callers who contact more than 250,000 alumni within a calendar year. I worked with a random sample of about 20,000 alumni drawn from this universe. Each person was called within the 10 months preceding my analysis.

I was particularly interested in variables that were related to these outcomes:

- the percentage of pledges versus refusals for the last call made to the person,

- the percentage of pledges made by check versus credit card, and

- the dollar amount of the pledge received.

The mean (average) pledge dollar amount per person called was slightly more than $33. The overall picture for the other outcomes for the entire sample appears in Figures 8.1 and 8.2. Figure 8.1 shows that 61 percent of the alumni refused to make any pledge on the last call, while 28 percent made a pledge. The remaining 11 percent gave a response (such as "call back") that motivated the caller (or call-center manager) to make no further attempts. Figure 8.2

Figure 8.1. Alumni response to latest call

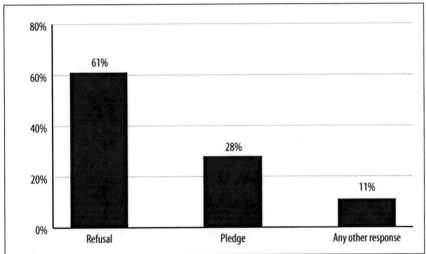

Figure 8.2. Payment method for pledges

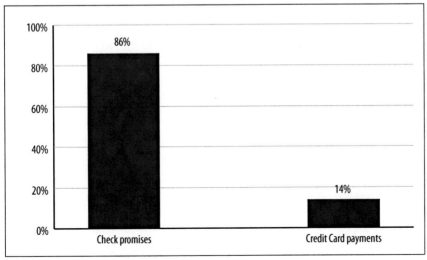

shows that most of the pledges (86 percent) were promises to send a check to the school; only 14 percent were credit card payments. (Obviously, the institution would prefer a credit card payment because that obviates any concern about fulfillment of the pledge.)

I then delved further to try to identify characteristics that correlated with these outcomes. I want to be clear that this is one exploratory study in an area crying out for comprehensive research, and what I say may not hold up when studies are done at other schools with better variables and better experimental designs than I was able to use here. That said, I think I uncovered three factors that are probably strongly related to whether a given call yields a pledge, the size of the pledge, and whether or not the caller is able to get a credit card payment for the pledge:

- who is called,

- the experience of the caller, and

- how long the call lasts.

Who is called

This factor should come as no big surprise. All the call-center workers I've ever talked to segment the alumni being called by certain variables, including how much the person has previously given when called for a pledge. That's certainly the case for the university whose data I used here.

To simplify matters, I divided the sample of 20,000 alumni into four groups roughly equal in size:

- those who had given nothing at all by phone,

- those who had given between $1 and $169,

- those who had given between $170 and $599, and

- those who had given $600 or more.

As you can see in Figure 8.3, there is a strong relationship between how much alumni had given by phone in the past and their pledge rate for this study. Those alumni who had previously given $600 or more were almost three times as likely to make a pledge as alumni who had never given by phone (43 percent versus 15 percent).

Figure 8.4 gives us a different (but corroborative) view of the relationship between previous phone giving and pledging. If anything, the relationship looks even more pronounced than it does in Figure 8.3. Notice that the mean (average) pledge for alumni who have given at least $600 is more than six times greater than the mean pledge for alumni who've given nothing previously.

Figure 8.3. Alumni response to latest call by total dollars given on previous calls

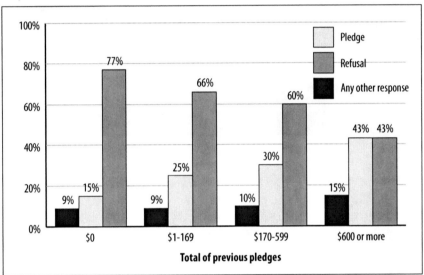

Figure 8.4. Mean pledge amount by total dollars given on previous calls

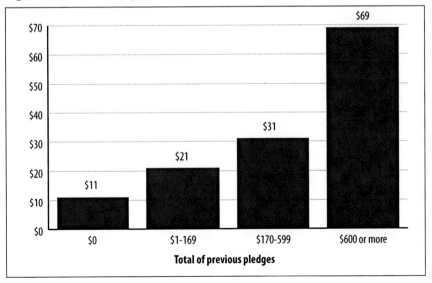

Figure 8.5. Mean credit card payment by total dollars given on previous calls

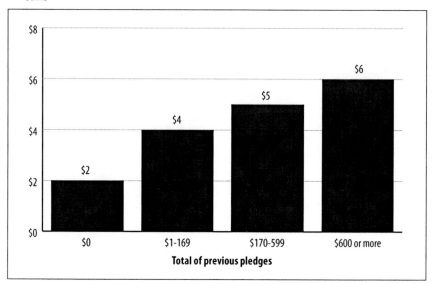

Lest we get too carried away, however, let's look at the mean credit card payment by previous giving. When we divide the total amount of pledges paid by credit card by the number of alumni in each previous giving group, we get the results you see in Figure 8.5. Two things seem to jump out from this graph: One, the average credit card payment (regardless of the previous giving group) is quite meager. Two, the differences among the groups are far less impressive than in Figure 8.4. It may be a lot easier to get a promise of a check from the $600-or-more group than from the $0 group. But that's clearly not the case for a credit card payment.

Caller experience

To get a measure of caller experience, I computed the number of calls each caller had made during the period of this study. Those who had made 400 calls or more I designated as "most experienced callers." Everyone else I labeled "least experienced callers." Admittedly, this is a pretty crude measure, but given the data I had to work with, I was at a loss to come up with anything better.

Figure 8.6 shows pretty clearly that the most experienced callers were considerably better than the least experienced callers at getting pledges and at not getting refusals. But, again, let's hold on a moment.

Figure 8.6. Alumni response by caller experience

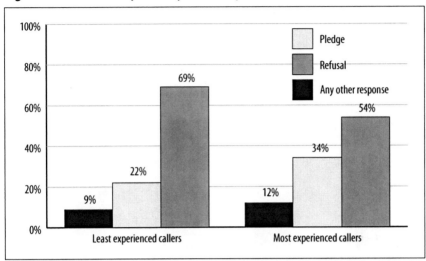

Figure 8.7. Mean pledge amount by total dollars given on previous calls and caller experience

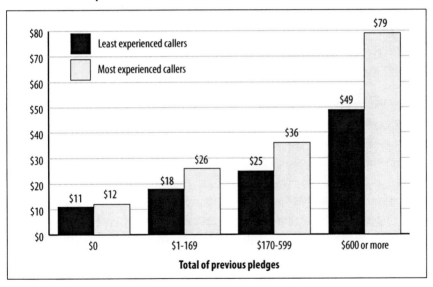

In Figure 8.7, we see the mean (average) pledge by caller experience broken out by the person's level of previous giving. It appears that the most experienced callers are better than the least experienced callers at getting bigger pledges from alumni who have given $600 or more previously. But how do these two groups

Figure 8.8. Mean credit card payment by total dollars given on previous calls and caller experience

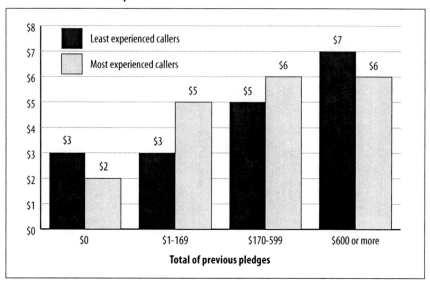

of callers compare when it comes to alumni who've never given before? They look pretty much the same. And when we look at Figure 8.8, we see that the credit card payments the two experience groups get are about the same regardless of the level of previous giving.

How long the call lasts

Given all the data that call centers collect, it's easy to measure the length of each call. I was particularly interested in how pledge making was related to how long the caller stayed on the phone. I divided the length of all calls into six groups. (You can see these groupings at the bottom of Figure 8.9.) From Figure 8.9 it's pretty obvious that the longer the call lasts (up to a certain point, of course) the greater the chances of getting a pledge, and the lower the chances of getting a refusal.

That's sort of what I expected to see. However, I was a little surprised to see what emerged from Figure 8.10. Notice how the chances of getting a credit card payment go up rather dramatically if the call lasts longer than three minutes.

Now let's look at Figures 8.11 and 8.12. Figure 8.11 shows the mean (average) pledge that least and most experienced callers got by length of call from alumni who had previously given $600 or more. Figure 8.12 shows the mean (average) pledge that least and most experienced callers got by length of call from alumni who had previously given nothing.

Figure 8.9. Alumni response by length of call

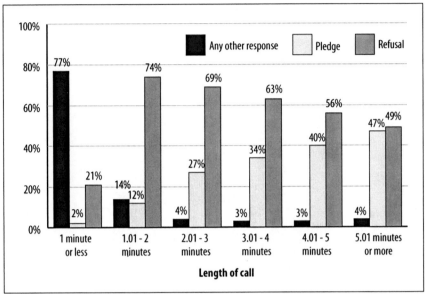

Figure 8.10. Payment method for pledges by length of call

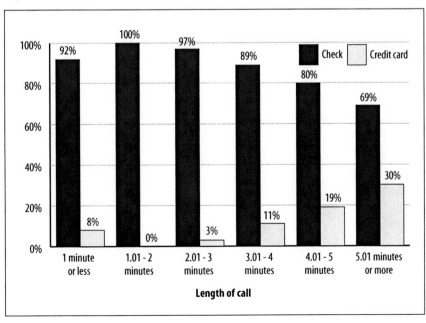

Figure 8.11. Mean pledge amount by caller experience and length of call for alumni who have given $600 or more on previous calls

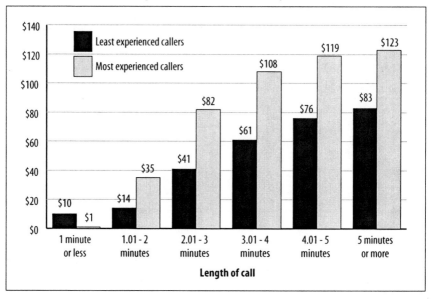

Figure 8.12. Mean pledge amount by caller experience and length of call for alumni who have not given on previous calls

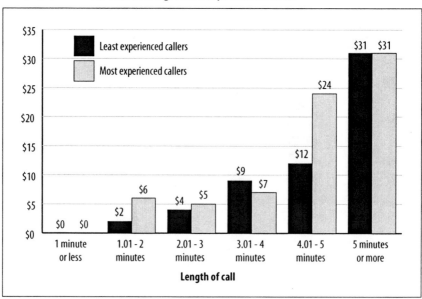

What do we have here? With alumni who've previously given $600 or more, the most experienced callers are more successful than the least experienced callers. We already know that. But the big thing that stands out is the dramatic rise in pledge amounts as the length of the call goes on, regardless of the experience of the caller.

Figure 8.12 also shows us something we already know: With alumni who have never given a pledge by phone before, the least experienced callers get about the same level of pledge as the most experienced callers. Experience doesn't seem to be the key factor with this group. The key factor seems to be how long the call lasts.

Some conclusions

I believe that science (especially the kind of applied science that has always fascinated me) is an incremental process. No one study is definitive. Groups of studies that build on and challenge each other are the stuff of which good theory and good practice are built. So nobody should gallop off with what I've reported here and dramatically start changing how they run their call centers. And I'm not worried that anyone will do that.

What I am worried about, however, is that those of us involved in educational advancement (be it secondary school, college, or university) won't start acting more scientific about our fundraising efforts. The data are there, and the resources and the good minds are there to do it. This little study is a case in point. I hope it encourages you to think about replicating it in your own call center. I hope it encourages you to think what implications the study might have for who you hire for your call center and how you train them. I even hope it encourages you to question what I've reported—to find holes in it and come up with something that's more enlightening.

Chapter 9

Whom the Screeners Can Find

*Can you predict which names on your prospect
list will yield data during wealth screening?*

Author's note: *I wrote this paper in 2007, shortly before we put this book to
bed. I don't hold back here. I say we can start making pretty accurate predictions
for any given school about the alumni for which an electronic screener will likely
find wealth-capacity data, and those for which they'll be unlikely to find such
information. My hope in writing this piece was not only to identify predictors of
"findability" but also to call attention to the fact that all of us in higher-education
advancement (users and vendors alike) should be studying the problem of how
hard it is to find wealth information on alumni. Right now, we have a tendency
to either accept or ignore the problem, not study it. That needs to change.*

ELECTRONIC WEALTH SCREENING. It's a big business in the general
field of advancement and certainly in the field of university advancement. If
you work in prospect research in a higher-education institution, you probably
(1) have been involved with a screening at some point, (2) are right in the midst
of one, or (3) are planning to do one in the not-too-distant future.

And let's be frank: Screening is not only a big business, it's a tough business. Most of us know that it's downright hard for a screener to take thousands
and thousands of names and accurately assess each person's capacity to make
a large gift to your school. Moreover, we know it's hard for screeners to find *any*
useful wealth data on lots of the names they receive. The percentages vary all
over the map, but it's not uncommon for a screener to come up empty on half
the names.

Why? Most of the reasons I only vaguely understand because I'm not an
expert on screening. But it's safe to say that finding out someone's exact wealth

is difficult unless that information is a matter of public record (for example, as it is for some high-level elected officials).

All that said, I've been very curious about whether there's some way a school could predict the names for which a screener would be *more* likely to find useful wealth information and those for which they would be *less* likely to find useful information. We know that the information in an alumni database can be used to make accurate predictions about a person's likelihood of giving to his or her alma mater. Why couldn't we use some of that same kind of information to predict whether a screener will turn up a useful wealth estimate for the same person?

Recently I was able to pull together enough data to make some positive steps toward answering this question. Here's what this article will cover:

- the data I examined,

- the findings that emerged from the data,

- making sense out of the findings, and

- some additional thoughts.

The data I examined

To address this issue, I needed some specific data—data that met the following criteria.

- **The data had to come from at least three institutions.** I felt this was a bare-minimum number of institutions from which I could even begin to draw some conclusions. I found three such schools. They are very different from one another. One is a large public higher-education institution out West. One is a private liberal arts institution in the Midwest. And the third is a faith-based institution in the South.

- **The data had to exist in each institution's alumni database before names were submitted to a screener.** I thought this was essential. What I didn't want was a situation where the school had specifically gathered certain kinds of data on records in *anticipation* of the screening. I wanted to know whether data already available in the database could be used to predict "findability."

- **The data from each had to include an overall indicator of wealth found for at least 25 percent of the names during a screening.** If you've done a screening, you know that screeners provide lots of fields when they return a set of names to you. Although many of these fields (like stock options and annual salary) sound intriguing and would be great to have information on, most of them are sparsely populated—they might be filled in for only a dozen names or less. While the information on a few names may be very useful for prospect research purposes, the numbers are not big enough to do sound statistical analyses.

- **The data had to include at least four fields or variables (common to all the institutions) that I could use as possible predictors of findability.** This turned out to be an easy criterion to meet. I found four such variables that seem strongly related to whether a screener can come up with useful wealth information about a graduate.

In order to protect the identity of the three institutions as well as the screeners, I need to be somewhat vague about the screening data I looked at. However, I can reveal these details:

- The number of records screened for each of the institutions was more than 8,000.

- All three screenings were done within the last five years.

- The variable I used to determine the match rate (the percentage of alumni on whom wealth data were found) for each had a title that included a word like "total" or "overall" or "combined"—one that conveyed a comprehensive estimate of an individual's "hard asset" financial resources.

- The variable I used to determine the match rate was *not* any kind of prediction or estimate of what the individual would give to the institution.

The findings that emerged from the data

The first thing I noticed about the data was how the three institutions differed in terms of match rates:

- School A had a match rate of just under 65 percent.

- School B had a match rate of about 42 percent.

- School C had a match rate of about 26 percent.

Schools A and B seemed rather typical of what I had seen over the years. School C was much lower than I had seen previously. I have no solid explanation for this difference. Perhaps the screener for School C used a different kind of matching logic than the screeners for the other two did. Maybe state differences in privacy laws account for the difference. Since this was only an exploratory study, I eventually stopped worrying about the difference and forged ahead.

For the three schools, I found four simple variables that differentiated between alumni whose wealth the screeners were able to find and alumni whose wealth the screeners were *not* able to find:

- whether or not a home telephone number was listed for the record,

- the gender of the person,

- whether or not the person had made a gift to the school, and

- whether or not the record had a prefix of "Ms." in the prefix or salutation field.

We'll start with the home telephone data. In Figures 9.1–9.3, it's obvious the screeners had much better luck in finding the wealth of alumni whose home phone number was listed in the database than they did with alumni whose home phone number was *not* listed. For School A, the screener was able to find wealth data on 76 percent of the alumni who had a home phone listed in the database, but only on 53 percent of alumni who did not have a home phone

Figure 9.1. Percentage of School A alumni whose wealth was found, by whether record included home phone

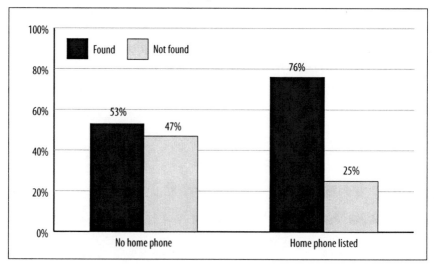

Figure 9.2. Percentage of School B alumni whose wealth was found, by whether record included home phone

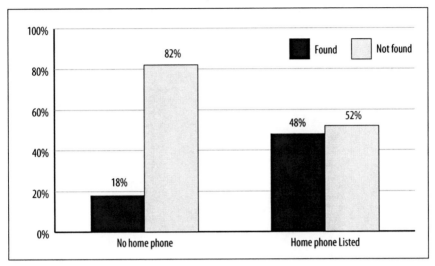

Figure 9.3. Percentage of School C alumni whose wealth was found, by whether record included home phone

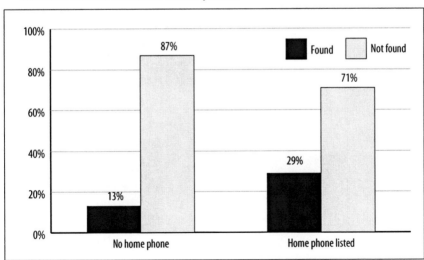

listed in the database. The difference was equally pronounced for Schools B and C.

The gender data are not as impressive as the home phone data, but Figures 9.4–9.6 show that screeners were more likely to find wealth data for men than

Figure 9.4. Percentage of School A alumni whose wealth was found, by gender

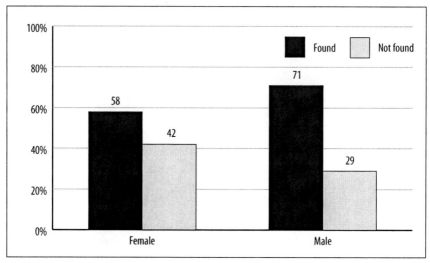

Figure 9.5. Percentage of School B alumni whose wealth was found, by gender

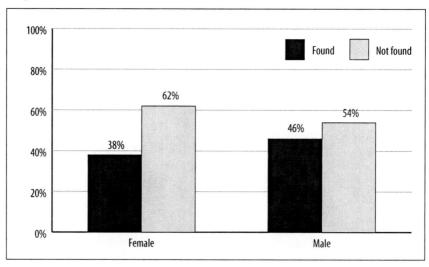

for women. Figure 9.4 shows that at School A, the find rate was 71 percent for men and 58 percent for women. Figure 9.5 shows a somewhat less impressive difference between the genders for School B: 46 percent for men and 38 percent for women. Figure 9.6 shows there wasn't much difference in the find rates for

Figure 9.6. Percentage of School C alumni whose wealth was found, by gender

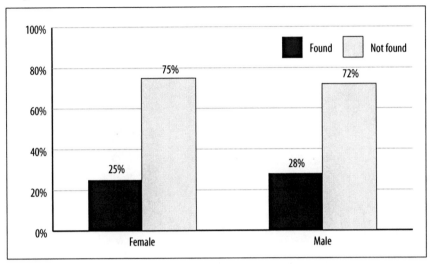

Figure 9.7. Percentage of School A alumni whose wealth was found, by giving history

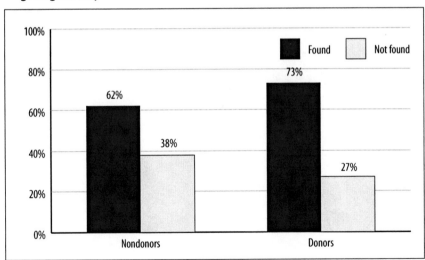

men and for women: 28 percent versus 25 percent. However, the difference was still in favor of the men.

Figures 9.7–9.9 show the find rates for alumni who had given anything to their schools versus alumni who had given nothing at all. It's pretty clear

Figure 9.8. Percentage of School B alumni whose wealth was found, by giving history

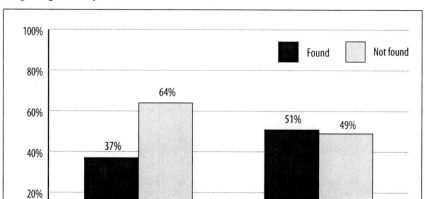

Figure 9.9. Percentage of School C alumni whose wealth was found, by giving history

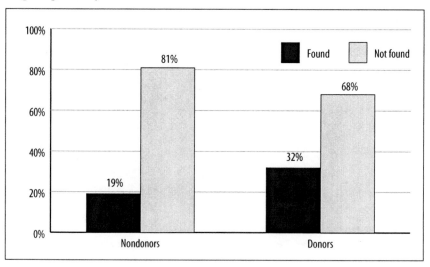

that it was easier for the screeners to find wealth data on donors than on nondonors.

Finally, let's look at the difference in find rates between alumni who have a prefix of "Ms." in the database versus all other alumni regardless of their prefix.

Figure 9.10. Percentage of School A alumni whose wealth was found, by prefix listed in record

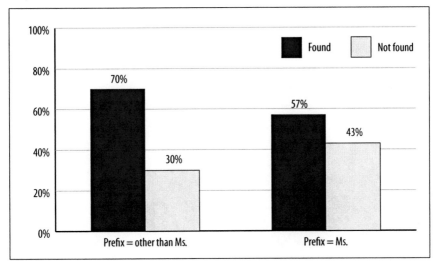

Figure 9.11. Percentage of School B alumni whose wealth was found, by prefix listed in record

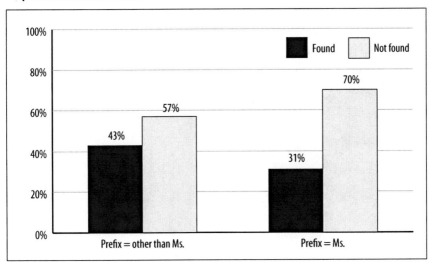

Figures 9.10–9.12 are clear: Screeners had a tougher time finding wealth estimates for alumni whose prefix was "Ms." than they did for alumni whose prefix was not "Ms."

Figure 9.12. Percentage of School C alumni whose wealth was found, by prefix listed in record

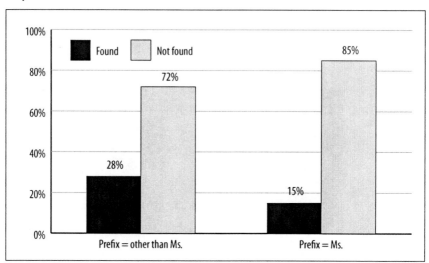

Making sense out of the findings

What do we make of all these data—the relationships between these four variables and whether a screener can find wealth on alumni? Perhaps more importantly, to what use might we put these findings?

To answer this second question, I did a little experiment with the data from School A, which had the highest match rate of the three schools. I asked what would happen if we were to create a simple score from the four variables:

- whether or not a home telephone number was listed for the record,

- the gender of the person,

- whether or not the person had made a gift to the school, and

- whether or not the record had a prefix of "Ms." in the prefix or salutation field.

Would that score show big differences between the find rates for alumni with low scores and alumni with high scores? The basic formula for the score was this:

SCORE = "HOME PHONE LISTED" + "MALE" + "HAVE GIVEN" + "PREFIX = OTHER THAN MS." + 1

Figure 9.13. Percentage of School A alumni whose wealth was found, by score level

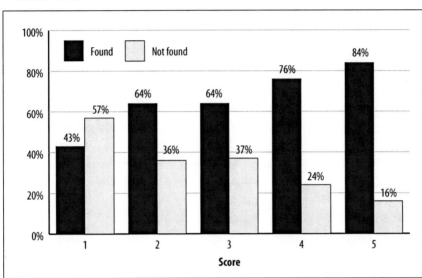

Here's what that means in plain English:

- If the record had a home phone listed, the record got a 1; otherwise a 0.

- If the person was male, the record got a 1; otherwise a 0.

- If the person had given anything at all to the school, the record got a 1; otherwise a 0.

- If the person did not have a prefix of "Ms.," the record got a 1; otherwise a 0.

- All records received a 1 to ensure there were no 0 scores.

- Scores ranged from 1 to 5. (For more information on constructing this kind of score, see Chapter 4, "A Simple Score.")

Figure 9.13 shows the find rates for alumni by score level. Clearly there's a very strong relationship between this simple little score and whether the screener could find useful wealth information on alumni. (The relationship for the other two schools looks very similar to what you see here.)

In looking at the data for this article, I found lots of other variables that predicted findability for individual schools other than the four variables I've presented here. Here, I was looking for commonality across schools and an uncomplicated way to get my message across. So, getting back to the question of how we might we use these data, I think it's very likely we could make pretty accurate predictions for any given school about which records are likely to yield wealth capacity in a screening, and which records are unlikely to do so.

Of course, there's a related question: Is trying to predict the easy-to-find versus hard-to-find alumni a worthwhile task for major gift professionals to undertake? I happen to think it is. Screening is time-consuming, and it's not inexpensive. Why spend a lot of time and money trying to gather capacity ratings for people who won't be found? That's like having the students in your call center make calls to alumni whom your data say you won't be able to reach, much less convince to give you a pledge. It just doesn't make good sense.

Some additional thoughts

Here are a couple of questions I'd like to pose, and for which I offer my own brief answers:

Why haven't we seen something like this little study before? I don't think there's anything earth-shaking about what I've laid out here. It just isn't very surprising that it's easier to find wealth-capacity information on someone whose home phone you have listed in your database than on someone whose phone number you don't have. The same is true for whether a person has given to your school before. This is common sense. But why haven't we seen these kinds of facts presented before this? Maybe they have been, and I just didn't get the news. But I doubt it. I think the problem is that as a profession, we don't study our data and what they can tell us about how to do advancement better. We don't have a tradition of hard-nosed applied science in our field. And that's got to change.

Is the way wealth screening gets done about to change? I think it is. As of this writing, I've recently returned from the 2007 meeting in Chicago of the Association of Professional Researchers for Advancement (APRA). As always, it was a stimulating experience—a chance to peek around the corner and see what's coming. I think one of the things that's coming is a more comprehensive and richer way to do wealth screenings. It looks like we'll be using the Web a lot more than we do now; as I write this, people are probably developing software that will allow you to submit a name to a very sophisticated Web search that will yield huge amounts of information boiled down in a way that will tell not only if you've found the right person (a big problem right now) but also the person's wealth and philanthropic interests. I don't expect this software and the service that delivers it to be cheap, at least not in the beginning. But I think it will soon render what I've written here as quaint and outdated as a rotary phone. We'll see.

About the Author

PETER B. WYLIE, ED.D., is a nationally recognized industrial psychologist and data analyst who teaches advancement professionals how to mine donor databases to find predictors of giving. Peter has been helping fundraising professionals with data mining for almost a decade. He is the author of *KeyDonor*, a CD-based interactive multimedia course in data mining, and the book *Data Mining for Fund Raisers* (CASE, 2004), both available online at *www.case.org/ books*. He is co-author (with Mardy Grothe) of *Can This Partnership Be Saved? Improving (or Salvaging) Your Key Business Relationships* (Upstart Publishing, 1993), *Problem Employees: How to Improve Their Performance* (Upstart Publishing, 1991), and *Problem Bosses: Who They Are and How to Deal with Them* (Fawcett, 1987). Peter has been allied with Data Description, Inc. for over two years in producing a data-mining multimedia training product, offering phone- and Web-delivered training courses, and providing predictive modeling and data-mining services to academic institutions and nonprofit organizations.

Printed in the United States
201960BV00004B/124-150/P